I0867370

Common Standards for K-12 Education?

Considering the Evidence

SUMMARY OF A WORKSHOP SERIES

Alexandra Beatty, Rapporteur

Committee on State Standards in Education:
A Workshop Series

Center for Education

Division of Behavioral and Social Sciences and Education

NATIONAL RESEARCH COUNCIL
OF THE NATIONAL ACADEMIES

THE NATIONAL ACADEMIES PRESS
Washington, D.C.
www.nap.edu

THE NATIONAL ACADEMIES PRESS 500 Fifth Street, N.W. Washington, DC 20001

NOTICE: The project that is the subject of this report was approved by the Governing Board of the National Research Council, whose members are drawn from the councils of the National Academy of Sciences, the National Academy of Engineering, and the Institute of Medicine. The members of the committee responsible for the report were chosen for their special competences and with regard for appropriate balance.

This study was supported by a contract between the National Academy of Sciences and the James B. Hunt, Jr. Institute for Educational Leadership and Policy. Any opinions, findings, conclusions, or recommendations expressed in this publication are those of the author(s) and do not necessarily reflect the views of the organizations or agencies that provided support for the project.

International Standard Book Number-13: 978-0-309-12524-6
International Standard Book Number-10: 0-309-12524-3

Additional copies of this report are available from National Academies Press, 500 Fifth Street, N.W., Lockbox 285, Washington, DC 20055; (800) 624-6242 or (202) 334-3313 (in the Washington metropolitan area); Internet, http://www.nap.edu.

Printed in the United States of America

Suggested citation: National Research Council. (2008). *Common Standards for K-12 Education?: Considering the Evidence: Summary of a Workshop Series.* Alexandra Beatty, Rapporteur. Committee on State Standards in Education: A Workshop Series. Center for Education, Division of Behavioral and Social Sciences and Education. Washington, DC: The National Academies Press.

THE NATIONAL ACADEMIES

Advisers to the Nation on Science, Engineering, and Medicine

The **National Academy of Sciences** is a private, nonprofit, self-perpetuating society of distinguished scholars engaged in scientific and engineering research, dedicated to the furtherance of science and technology and to their use for the general welfare. Upon the authority of the charter granted to it by the Congress in 1863, the Academy has a mandate that requires it to advise the federal government on scientific and technical matters. Dr. Ralph J. Cicerone is president of the National Academy of Sciences.

The **National Academy of Engineering** was established in 1964, under the charter of the National Academy of Sciences, as a parallel organization of outstanding engineers. It is autonomous in its administration and in the selection of its members, sharing with the National Academy of Sciences the responsibility for advising the federal government. The National Academy of Engineering also sponsors engineering programs aimed at meeting national needs, encourages education and research, and recognizes the superior achievements of engineers. Dr. Charles M. Vest is president of the National Academy of Engineering.

The **Institute of Medicine** was established in 1970 by the National Academy of Sciences to secure the services of eminent members of appropriate professions in the examination of policy matters pertaining to the health of the public. The Institute acts under the responsibility given to the National Academy of Sciences by its congressional charter to be an adviser to the federal government and, upon its own initiative, to identify issues of medical care, research, and education. Dr. Harvey V. Fineberg is president of the Institute of Medicine.

The **National Research Council** was organized by the National Academy of Sciences in 1916 to associate the broad community of science and technology with the Academy's purposes of furthering knowledge and advising the federal government. Functioning in accordance with general policies determined by the Academy, the Council has become the principal operating agency of both the National Academy of Sciences and the National Academy of Engineering in providing services to the government, the public, and the scientific and engineering communities. The Council is administered jointly by both Academies and the Institute of Medicine. Dr. Ralph J. Cicerone and Dr. Charles M. Vest are chair and vice chair, respectively, of the National Research Council.

www.national-academies.org

COMMITTEE ON STATE STANDARDS IN EDUCATION: A WORKSHOP SERIES

LORRAINE McDONNELL (*Chair*), Department of Political Science, University of California, Santa Barbara
THOMAS B. CORCORAN, Consortium for Policy Research and Education, Teacher's College, Columbia University
ROBERT LINN, Department of Education (emeritus), University of Colorado, Boulder
WILLIAM TATE, Department of Arts and Sciences, Washington University in St. Louis
LAURESS WISE, Human Resources Research Organization, Monterey, CA
KAREN WIXSON, School of Education, University of Michigan

STUART ELLIOTT, Co-study Director
LISA TOWNE, Co-study Director
ALEXANDRA BEATTY, Senior Program Officer
MARGARET HILTON, Senior Program Officer
KELLY DUNCAN, Program Assistant

Preface

Standards-based accountability has become a central feature of the public education system in each state and is a theme of national discussions about how achievement for all students can be improved and achievement gaps narrowed. Questions remain, however, about the implementation of standards and accountability systems and about whether their potential benefits have been fully realized. Each of the 50 states has adopted its own set of standards, and though there is overlap among them, there is also wide variation in the ways states have devised and implemented their systems. This variety may have both advantages and disadvantages, but it nevertheless raises a fundamental question: Is the establishment of common K-12 academic standards, which states could voluntarily adopt, the logical next step for standards-based reform?

The National Research Council, with support from the James B. Hunt, Jr. Institute for Educational Leadership and Policy, sponsored a set of workshops to examine the possibilities for common standards. The goal of this project was not to answer the policy question of whether or not common standards would be a good idea. Rather, the goal was to provide an objective look at the available evidence regarding the ways in which standards are currently functioning, the strategies that might be used to pursue common standards, and the issues that doing so might present. The workshops were planned by the Committee on State Standards in Education, whose membership reflects diverse policy and research perspectives.

The workshop series focused first on the role that standards have been playing in the states, and included a review of the policy and research context in which current standards-based reform efforts are operating, a consideration of how the costs of standards and accountability systems might be calculated, and an analysis of similarities and differences among states' content and performance standards. The second workshop addressed possible options for establishing common education standards, criteria for evaluating different approaches, and the tradeoffs that this course might entail, as viewed from a variety of perspectives. This report summarizes the presentations and discussions from both workshops, which were held in January and March 2008.[1]

This workshop summary has been reviewed in draft form by individuals chosen for their diverse perspectives and technical expertise, in accordance with procedures approved by the Report Review Committee of the National Research Council. The purpose of this independent review is to provide candid and critical comments that will assist the institution in making its published report as sound as possible and to ensure that the report meets institutional standards for objectivity, evidence, and responsiveness to the charge. The review comments and draft manuscript remain confidential to protect the integrity of the process. We thank the following individuals for their review of this report: Julie Bell, Education Program, National Conference of State Legislature, Denver, CO; Suellen Reed, Department of Public Instruction, Indianapolis Department of Education; Barbara Reys, Learning Teaching and Curriculum, University of Missouri; and Lori Taylor, The Bush School of Government and Public Service, Texas A&M University.

Although the reviewers listed above provided many constructive comments and suggestions, they were not asked to endorse the content of the report, nor did they see the final draft of the report before its release. The review of this report was overseen by Diana C. Pullin, Lynch School of Education, Boston College. Appointed by the National Research Council, she was responsible for making certain that an independent examination of this report was carried out in accordance with institutional procedures and that all review comments were carefully considered. Responsibility for the final content of this report rests entirely with the author and the institution.

The committee would also like to thank the co-study directors of this project, Stuart Elliott and Lisa Towne, for their leadership throughout;

[1]A report summarizing the first workshop was published shortly after it was held so that the material covered could be made available as quickly as possible. This second report is designed to supersede that report; much of the text from that report is thus repeated or modified here. The first report, *Assessing the Role of K-12 Academic Standards in the States Workshop Summary*, is available at http://www.nap.edu/catalog.php?record_id=12207.

Margaret Hilton for her help in planning and organizing both workshops; Alix Beatty for drafting both reports; and Kelly Duncan for excellent logistical support. We also gratefully acknowledge the contributions of report editors Genie Grohman and Christine McShane, and report review officer Kirsten Sampson Snyder. Last but not least, the committee extends sincere thanks to Judith Rizzo and her colleagues at the Hunt Institute for their support and advice throughout the process.

Lorraine McDonnell, *Chair*
Committee on State Standards in
Education: A Workshop Series

Contents

1 INTRODUCTION 1

2 CONSIDERING THE STATUS QUO 5
Views from the States, 5
Variability in Content and Performance Standards and Assessments, 11
Paradoxes, 25

3 CONSIDERING THE OPTIONS 27

4 ANALYZING QUALITY AND IMPACT 31
Quality of Content Standards, 31
Impact of Standards on Teaching and Learning, 34

5 COSTS 39
Cost Estimation Framework, 40
Applying the Framework in Three States, 42
Estimating the Cost of Educational Adequacy, 48

6 POLITICAL AND LEGAL CONSIDERATIONS 53
Political Feasibility, 53
Implications for Educational Adequacy Litigation, 55

7 PERSPECTIVES ON COMMON STANDARDS 59
Two Examples, 59
Researchers, 62
Elected Officials, 64
Implementers, 65

8 CONCLUDING REFLECTIONS 69
Synthesis, 69
Closing Thoughts, 72

REFERENCES 75

APPENDIXES

A January 2008 Workshop Agenda and Participants 77
B March 2008 Workshop Agenda and Participants 85

1

Introduction

Every state in the United States now has its own standards for education from kindergarten through grade 12, at least in core subjects. Some are based on content standards developed by professional societies in mathematics, English language arts, science, civics, foreign languages, and other academic subjects. Other organizations also have developed their own standards and benchmarks. For example, Mid-Continent Research for Education and Learning (McREL) offers standards developed with the goal of applying a consistent structure and degree of rigor and specificity to standards in diverse subjects (http://www.mcrel.org/standards-benchmarks/).

This abundance of standards reflects a vigorous response to the call for high standards articulated in the 1983 report *A Nation at Risk* (National Commission on Excellence in Education, 1983), and it also poses a variety of questions for educators, policy makers, and the public more than 20 years later. What role are these standards playing? What are the strengths and weaknesses of the reform efforts that have been anchored by these standards? How are these standards applied, and how might standards-based reforms be improved? Would a move toward national standards in core academic subjects lead to improved instruction and learning? How might common standards be developed? Would this approach be feasible? These questions were the stimulus for the workshop series summarized in this report.

Although the position that there should be a single set of academic standards in core subjects that states would be encouraged or required to adopt or closely model is not new, a number of groups have recently advocated it. The discussion surrounding renewal of the No Child Left Behind Act (NCLB) has focused new attention on the effects of the current model, in which states independently develop standards that vary widely in focus and content. As Judith Rizzo of the James B. Hunt, Jr. Institute for Educational Leadership and Policy noted in explaining the impetus for the workshop series, NCLB has shone a "spotlight on the incredible variability of state test scores, both within and among states." The variation in student performance has caused many to wonder whether the logical next step for a nation committed to improving achievement for all students is to move toward common standards.

The Commission on No Child Left Behind, the Education Trust, the Fordham Foundation, and the American Federation of Teachers are among those who have argued in favor of voluntary national, or common, standards as a means of improving both achievement and equity (Goertz, 2007; Massell, 2008). Others have argued against common standards on the grounds that states, school districts, and teachers need flexibility to serve their students' needs and that reaching consensus on the shape and content of common standards—and even on a workable process for establishing that consensus—would be a formidable challenge. Complicating the discussion is the fact that evaluations of existing state standards in core subjects by such groups as Editorial Projects in Education, the Fordham Foundation, and the American Federation of Teachers have found many of them wanting (American Federation of Teachers, 2003; Editorial Projects in Education, 2008; Gross et al., 2005). A further complication is the fact that the term "standards" is used in a somewhat imprecise way. In the context of the workshops it was generally used to refer to both content standards, which describe material that students should be expected to learn, and performance standards, which describe the level of proficiency or mastery expected of them. Most state standards specify both.

To support analysis of these conflicting points of view, the committee wished first to examine the ways in which standards are currently functioning in the states and then to consider possible approaches to implementing common standards that could apply in all the states. Four questions guided the examination of the status quo:

1. What are the major roles that standards play in state K-12 education policy and practice?
2. What are the major strengths and weaknesses of K-12 state standards-based reform efforts with respect to achieving efficiency, equity, and quality? What are states doing to achieve these goals?
3. How and to what degree are the strengths and weaknesses of reform efforts related to the standards themselves? How and to

what degree have the standards changed other education policies in states?
4. How and to what degree are the strengths and weaknesses of reform efforts related to having unique state standards?

To structure the examination of possible approaches to the development and implementation of common standards, the committee developed an options and evaluation framework, which served two purposes. Highlighting the major dimensions along which standards systems might vary served both as a reminder of the principal elements in a thoughtful discussion of options and as a guide for thinking through the elements about which choice would be possible.

The report begins, in Chapter 2, with an overview of the current status of standards in the states, which includes a look at the views of policy makers from five states and analyses of the ways in which current standards vary across several dimensions. Chapter 3 provides greater detail about the options and evaluation framework developed by the committee. Chapter 4 discusses analysis of the quality of content standards and of the impact of standards on educational outcomes. Chapter 5 provides a framework for considering the cost implications of a move to common standards, as well as an estimate of those costs, and Chapter 6 explores the political feasibility of this policy and the implications such a move might have for legal rulings regarding educational adequacy. A range of perspectives on possibilities for common standards are explored in Chapter 7, which describes the views of several observers, as well as two examples of efforts to develop common standards, the New England Common Assessment Program and the American Diploma Project's Algebra II end-of-course exam. The final chapter is a synthesis of the key issues that surfaced in the two workshops. Appendix A contains the first workshop agenda and list of participants and Appendix B contains these materials for the second workshop.

2

Considering the Status Quo

Before considering options for integrating the most successful elements of standards-based systems into a common system, the committee wished to develop an accurate picture of the way the standards already in place are operating. A look at the views of policy makers in several states provided the basis for an overview of the evolution of the role of standards in the states and highlighted some of the key challenges that remain. Analysis of the content covered in state standards and of the performance expectations that states define provides a detailed picture of the extent of variation across the states.

VIEWS FROM THE STATES

The views of state-level policy makers were the first focus. Diane Massell (2008) analyzed for the committee a series of interviews with education policy makers in five states: California, Florida, Massachusetts, North Dakota, and Texas. The purpose of Massell's interviews was to solicit opinions from a range of experienced policy makers who have been engaged in standards-based education reform, the catchall term for measures that states have taken to improve instruction and learning by organizing both policy and practice around clear, measurable standards. Massell and her colleagues hoped to trace both common themes and insights and possible differences, as well as to flag views that may be developing in response to current events. The five states were chosen to reflect both geographical diversity and diversity of experience with standards. California, which initiated its standards approach during the 1980s, was an early adopter, for example, whereas North Dakota adopted standards in response to federal requirements in 1994. The 21 interview subjects included officials or education aides from governors' offices, members of state boards of education, state legislators, and state education agency officials.

Massell began with a brief overview of the evolution of standards-based reforms in the states. She highlighted the current, unprecedented degree of public engagement in the specifics of implementing standards-based systems, particularly attention on the curriculum and instruction that make them concrete. She described standards-based reform as having had the effect of "opening Pandora's box," because it resulted in a new transparency with regard to curriculum and instruction. Massell was borrowing a phrase from a 1950s report that described districts as reluctant to allow the public to involve itself with potentially divisive questions about what and how children should be taught.

Although the minimum competency movement of the 1970s—as well as lawsuits in a number of states intended to force states to equalize school funding—increased focus on schools' accountability to states with regard to what students actually learn, the achievement bar was set relatively low, Massell explained. The standards-based reform movement that developed in response to *A Nation at Risk* (National Commission on Excellence in Education, 1983) expanded the role of standards, emphasizing rigorous requirements for high school graduation. As national organizations, such as the National Council of Teachers of Mathematics (NCTM), as well as individual states began to put forward more detailed statements of what students should be expected to know and be able to do, the concept of systemic reform, suggested by Smith and O'Day (1991), sharpened the focus on how standards might lead to the desired learning. The logic of systemic reform was that the primary elements of an educational system—such as curriculum, instruction, teacher preparation, professional development, and assessment—must all be aligned to carefully developed content and performance standards in order for those standards to affect teaching and learning. In this view, educators would still retain significant flexibility in meeting expectations but be held accountable for the results.

In 1994 the reauthorization of the Elementary and Secondary Education Act made standards-based reform the official national approach to public schooling by requiring states to set challenging standards aligned to assessments and accountability measures (Massell, 2008). The testing requirements imposed by the No Child Left Behind Act (NCLB) of 2001 built on that commitment, requiring states to (1) publish challenging academic content standards in English/language arts and mathematics for each of grades 3 through 8 and one secondary grade, as well as standards for science in three grades, and to (2) assess students in these grades and subjects annually and to hold schools accountable for the results (http://www.ed.gov/policy/elsec/leg/esea02/index.html [April 2008]). Those requirements—and the consequences imposed by the law for failing to meet them—have meant that parents and others have a significantly increased interest in the precise content of standards, curriculum, the tests used to measure proficiency, and the material covered in classrooms.

Massell's interviews found intense differences of opinion related to standards. Her interview subjects reported disagreement about how rigorous academic and performance standards are and should be, about whether measures that sharpen accountability also lead to an unacceptable narrowing of the curriculum, and about the fairness of accountability sanctions.

Despite tension around a number of issues, Massell noted that the leaders she and her colleagues interviewed generally take standards-based reform and accountability for granted, viewing this approach as a "central framework guiding state education policy and practice." Even the leaders from North Dakota, where standards were adopted largely under federal duress, viewed this approach as a part of the landscape that is not likely to change. The other four states had made a stronger commitment to standards, and the leaders from those states described them in such terms as "even more central over time" and "integral" to policy initiatives. Massell observed that opening issues related to curriculum and instruction to public discussion has not had the effect of killing reform, as some may have feared, and the result has been "a surprising degree of agreement regarding the meaning and purpose of education."

The North Dakota respondents were more muted than the others, however. They were less likely to see standards as "central" to policy and tended to describe the effects of standards on classroom practice as marginal. Moreover, respondents from all five states reported that the focus on standards remains variable across and within both states and districts, as do their effects on instruction and learning.

Massell explained that the interviewers asked state education leaders for their impressions regarding several aspects of standards-based reform, such as its impact on practice, learning opportunities, the quality of education, and resources. The leaders' responses to these issues generated an array of reactions from workshop discussants and participants.

Equity

The effects of standards-based accountability systems on achievement gaps and equality of opportunity for disadvantaged students was the first specific topic discussed in the interviews. In general, Massell reported, the state leaders believe that standards-based reform has led to:

- greater awareness of and attention to the academic performance of disadvantaged students;
- the expectation that all students will meet rigorous standards;
- reductions in achievement gaps;
- a more uniform education system (within states); and
- instruction that is tailored to the needs of individual students.

They generally agreed that increased awareness of the performance of all groups may be the most widely recognized accomplishment of standards-based reform, and particularly of the NCLB legislation.

Yet both the interview subjects and the workshop participants recognized the challenges of increasing equity in education and the limitations of what has been accomplished. The gaps have not been eliminated, and most agreed that reductions thus far have been fairly modest. Massell noted that according to a study by the Center on Education Policy (2007), gaps in most states remain substantial despite reductions, and some states have seen no reductions. Urban schools—those with the largest proportions of disadvantaged students—are the least likely to be meeting NCLB performance targets. Discussant Brian Stecher reinforced the concern that improvement has been modest, pointing out that "under the threat of severe sanctions from No Child Left Behind, there is an unknown amount of inflation in test scores, and what we see in terms of gap closing on state tests is not always replicated in other low-stakes assessments." Many participants viewed the challenge of providing a truly equitable education for disadvantaged students as a central purpose of standards-based reform.

Capacity

The interview subjects viewed the states' capacity to carry out all the improvements envisioned in standards-based reform as the most significant challenge to improving equity and achieving its other goals, and workshop participants were quick to agree. The reforms have stretched state agencies and districts significantly during a period in which most have been losing personnel and resources. Massell noted that Massachusetts had 325 full-time staff when its reforms were enacted into law in 1993, although it had employed 990 just 13 years earlier. Smaller staffs have been responsible for developing new standards and aligning curriculum, instruction, and assessments to them. Other technical challenges, such as measuring the progress of English language learners in a valid manner, have increased the difficulty of implementing the intended reforms.

NCLB required support of Title I schools (those serving specified percentages of low-income children) in specific ways. As growing numbers of schools and districts fall short of the NCLB performance targets, the strains on personnel are increasing. Fully 25 percent of schools across the country fell short of adequate yearly progress targets in 2004-2005, and the numbers have been increasing since then, although Massell noted that that figure masks significant variation across states. For example, Florida and Alabama reported that as many as 67 percent of their schools and 90 percent of their districts would fall short in 2008. Moreover, many states project that a cascading number of schools will be identified as underperforming in the coming years, as the law's 2014 deadline for having 100 percent of students perform at proficient levels draws closer.

Capacity is critical to making a standards-based system perform as it is intended to. One necessary component of the strategy is data analysis, since, ideally, thoughtful analysis of timely data will guide teachers as they plan instruction; administrators as they plan teaching assignments, professional development, and many other aspects of their schools; and district and state staff as they make decisions about key questions, such as curriculum planning and resource allocation. Yet as Stecher and other discussants pointed out, teachers, administrators, and policy makers frequently lack either the training or the time—or both—to use the data they receive wisely. Few teachers have been adequately trained to use data to make improvements in instruction, and the annual testing data that are the most typical product of accountability systems are not particularly useful for that purpose.

More broadly, a number of participants stressed that standards-based accountability models provide a structure for identifying problems, but they do not directly address the challenges of bringing about better instruction. There is a risk that the standards-based reform model, and all of the testing and other time- and resource-intensive activities that are associated with it, may distract educators from one of the central challenges of reform: figuring out how to address the needs of disadvantaged students. As discussant Lynn Olson put it, one benefit of common standards could be to "force us to confront gross inequities," although educators and the public have known for decades that disadvantaged students are not doing well.

Quality

Building on the capacity issues, participants also discussed the gaps between the ideal model and reality. Olson noted that in the evaluation of state standards recently published by *Education Week*, not one state earned a top score on each of the criteria used, and many scored very poorly in a number of areas (Editorial Projects in Education, 2008). Stecher expanded on this point, arguing that very high standards are needed for the standards themselves. Because everything—including curriculum, textbooks, development of assessments, language for reporting results to the public—flows from the standards, they need not only to be clearly written and concise, but also to reflect current understanding of how children learn and their conceptual development. They also need to provide guidance about the performance criteria for determining whether students have mastered particular standards and guidance about the relative importance of the different elements included.

In practice, as the *Quality Counts* (Editorial Projects in Education, 2008) and other evaluations attest, state standards are not yet meeting those kinds of criteria. In the absence of the guidance that standards should provide, the default source for guidance is the assessment system. As Stecher put it: "We may be drifting toward assessment-based reform, rather than standards-based reform."

Yet the standards themselves may be the best developed aspect of the evolving reform systems. Participants called attention to persistent concerns about the nature, rigor, and quality of the assessments used in many states and about the narrowing effects they can have on curriculum and instruction. For example, few states systematically provide for extensive formative assessments that teachers could use to tailor instruction to individual students' needs. These kinds of concerns, many noted, suggest the potential benefits to states of greater uniformity among them. States could much more easily take advantage of one another's knowledge and experience and avoid duplication of effort if they were applying consistent frameworks.

This point was reinforced by questions about whether the multiple-standards model has yielded the consistency that was hoped for even within states. Researchers and policy makers from several states suggested that there is far more variation in both content and performance standards in practice than may be evident in states' written plans. As discussant Rae Ann Kelsch explained: "People are very reluctant to give up control." Although she spoke on the basis of the experience in North Dakota, which has not embraced standards wholeheartedly, others echoed her view. Standards-based systems have provided a model and a unifying conception of the purpose of education, "but very different goals can exist under the same banner," as one participant put it. Discussant Scott Montgomery said that the problem lies in changing the entire system, not just in unifying the standards, so for him common standards would not necessarily bring the changes that he believes are needed.

VARIABILITY IN CONTENT AND PERFORMANCE STANDARDS AND ASSESSMENTS

Similarities and differences among states' content and performance standards are key to understanding the extent to which any move toward more common standards would have a substantive impact on current standards-based systems. An examination of states' approaches was organized around three framing questions:

1. How and to what extent do K-12 state content standards in English/language arts, mathematics, and science at key grades vary?
2. How and to what extent do K-12 state performance standards in English/language arts, mathematics, and science at key grades vary?
3. How and to what extent does the implementation of K-12 state content and performance standards in multiple academic subjects in classrooms vary?

Analysis of both content and performance standards provided the foundation for an extensive discussion of these questions. Andrew Porter and his colleagues described a very detailed review of 31 states' standards in the three subjects, with a focus on grades 4 and 8, which was developed for the workshop. Michael Petrilli described an analysis conducted by the Fordham Foundation and the Northwest Evaluation Association to compare proficiency standards across states, and Peggy Carr described the results of an analysis by the National Center for Education Statistics of the relationship between proficiency standards for state assessments and those of the National Assessment of Educational Progress.[1]

Content Standards

Porter and his colleagues addressed the first question by analyzing state content standards in English/language arts/reading, mathematics, and science for grades K-8 (Porter, Polikoff, and Smithson, 2008). Their analysis was based on a conceptual framework for considering the primary influences on teachers' instructional practices. Their hypothesis was that teachers are most strongly influenced by standards policies that have five characteristics:

---

[1]The term "proficiency standards" refers to the level of performance identified on a particular test as the minimum that qualifies as "proficient." Thus, it is a type of performance standard.

1. They are specific in their messages to teachers about what they are to teach.
2. They are consistent (aligned) among themselves so that teachers receive a coherent message.
3. They have authority, in that they are developed and promoted by experts, are officially adopted by the state, are consistent with standards practice, and are promoted by charismatic individuals—meaning individuals who provide leadership and motivate those who must implement the standards.
4. They have power, in that compliance with them is rewarded, whereas failure to comply is sanctioned.
5. They have stability, in that they are kept in place over time.

The team also based their analysis on a methodology they developed for describing in detail what it is that teachers teach, which they call a three-dimensional content language. Although this methodology actually predated the standards-based reform movement, it has proved a useful tool for examining the content of state standards documents.

Porter described the method as a way of producing a visual representation of the relative coverage of various elements of a particular field that is similar to a topographical map of a geographical region. Using the content language, Porter and colleagues have divided each subject into general areas. For example, in mathematics there are 16 general areas (e.g., operations, measurement, basic algebra), and each of these can be further subdivided into between 9 and 14 more specific topics—for a total of 217. Apart from the subtopics that make up each field, the language also distinguishes levels of cognitive demand, which are also somewhat different for each subject. There are eight cognitive levels for mathematics: memorize, perform procedures, demonstrate understanding, conjecture, generalize, prove, solve novel problems, and make connections. Thus, Porter explained, content is defined as the intersection of these two dimensions. Using this tool one can determine, for example, not just whether or not linear equations are covered, but also whether students will be expected to memorize one, solve one, or use one to solve a story problem.

To apply this language analysis to a state's standards, trained analysts review and code the most specific available description of the standard for a particular subject and grade level. Each standard is analyzed by three to five analysts, and items that are difficult to code are flagged and discussed. The codes are entered into cells as proportions, with 0 representing no emphasis and 1 representing a very strong one. The cells are used to build the visual display that illustrates both the degree of focus on the various topics and the cognitive demand.

Porter and colleagues drew on data from 31 states, although not all provided data for every subject and grade level. The team also analyzed the national science standards and those of the NCTM. They focused on grades 4 and 8, with the goal of highlighting the degree to which states' standards showed overlap or conceptual progressions between those two grades. Having entered the codes, they were able to conduct a variety of analyses and comparisons.

For any pair of states for which they had data, the alignment for a particular standard can be calculated. Using averages of these results, they were also able to calculate alignment across and within grade levels.

Figure 2-1 presents a pair of coarse-grained content maps showing the results for the two states that are most aligned in English/language arts/reading for fourth grade. It is clear from the figure that content areas such as vocabulary, comprehension, and language study (the darkest areas) are strongly emphasized in both Ohio and Indiana and that neither state places any emphasis on phonemic awareness. These content areas, which

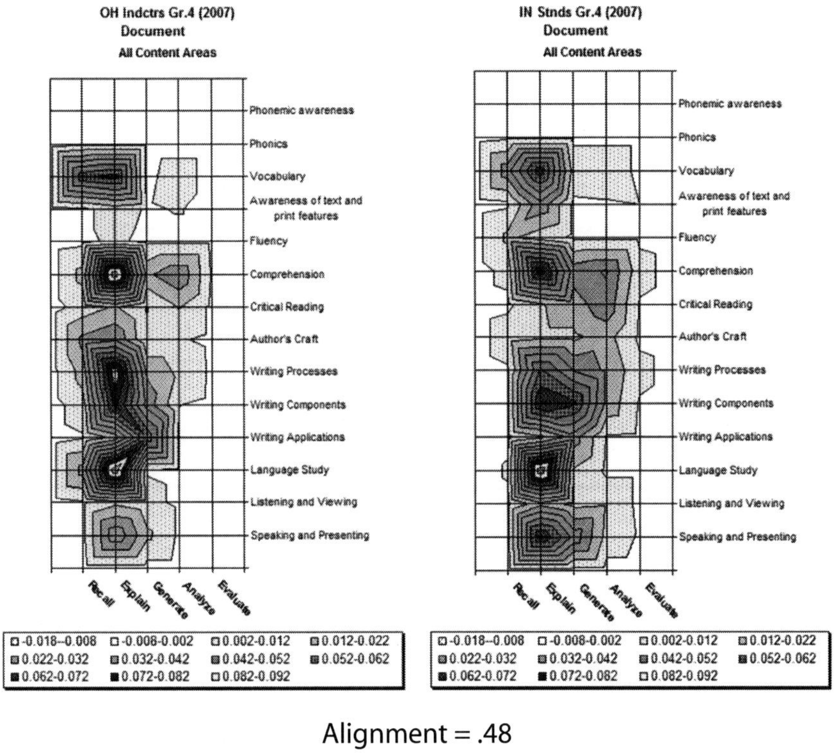

FIGURE 2-1 Coarse-grained content maps for English/language arts/reading for grade 4.
SOURCE: Porter, Polikoff, and Smithson (2008, Figure 1).

show up as darkest for both states, also line up along the column labeled "explain." This indicates that both states target the level of cognitive demand the researchers labeled as "explain" for these content areas. In other words, whichever areas show up as dark in the maps for both of the states being compared are ones that are emphasized in both states. One of the areas that showed up as strongly aligned for these two states, comprehension at the "explain" level of challenge, is shown in greater detail in the two fine-grained content maps in Figure 2-2. The subcategories of this instructional area—which include recognizing the meaning of words from the context; understanding of phrase, sentence, and paragraph; and the like—are mapped in the same way, according to degree of emphasis and cognitive level. This pair of maps shows, for example, that both Ohio and Indiana place strong emphasis on such strategies as activating prior

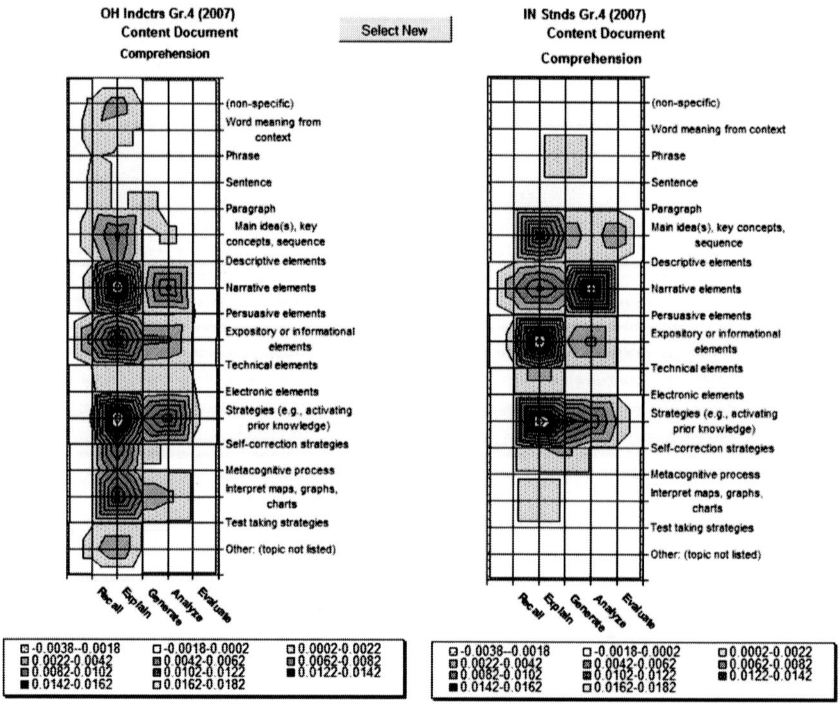

FIGURE 2-2 Fine-grained content maps for comprehension, English/language arts/reading for grade 4.
SOURCE: Porter, Polikoff, and Smithson (2008, Figure 22).

knowledge and that both associate the same degree of cognitive demand with this strand of the standard for reading comprehension.

The team also looked at the degree of alignment among 14 states in English/language arts/reading for grades 4 and 8, as shown in Table 2-1. The index runs from 0 to 1.00 with 1.00 representing perfect alignment. The results show significant variation, from lows, such as the .07 alignment between Maine and Wisconsin for grade 8, to highs, such as .47 between Ohio and California for grade 8. The researchers also examined the degree of alignment among the states' standards and the national science standards and the NCTM standards. Porter and colleagues (2008) have produced a voluminous body of data: 90 figures, 10 tables, and an appendix; this material and further detail about their analysis can be found in their paper.[2]

Porter explained that although it would be much easier if these data could be simplified, he and his colleagues could find no substitute for the fine-grained analysis for answering the questions at hand. Nevertheless, some key general points were evident. First, they found little evidence to support the hypothesis that there is a de facto national curriculum. The degree of variability they found across states, and between state and national standards, does not support that hypothesis. In fact, they found that the alignment of topic coverage within states from grade to grade (the degree of overlap in what is in the standards for each grade, as students ideally progress) is generally greater than the degree of alignment across states in the material they cover at particular grades. The repetition, Porter suggested, sends students the message: "Don't you dare learn this the first time we teach it; otherwise you are going to be bored out of your skull in the subsequent grades."

Porter and colleagues did find some indication that a few core areas are covered more consistently across states than the overall alignment data would show—or a small de facto common core curriculum. However, they also concluded that states' content standards are in general not focused on a few big ideas. Although the states vary in this as well, overall their standards do not demonstrate the clear focus and discipline that many have advocated.

State Assessments

Assessing the extent to which the performance standards that states set come close to defining a de facto common standard for proficiency was the impetus behind another study, described by Michael Petrilli.

[2]The material is available at http://www7.nationalacademies.org/cfe/State_Standards_Workshop_1_Agenda.html [May 2008].

TABLE 2-1 State-to-State Alignment, 4th and 8th Grade Standards for English/Language Arts/Reading

	CA Stnds Gr.4	DE GLEs Gr.4	ID Stnds Gr.4	IN Stnds Gr.4	KS Stnds Gr.4	ME GLEs Gr.4	MN ELAR Stnds. Gr.4	MT R Stnds Gr.4	NH Reading GLEs Gr.4	OH Indctrs Gr.4	OK Stnds Gr.4	OR Stnds Gr.4	VT GLEs Gr.4	WI Stnds Gr.4
CA Stnds Gr.4 (2005)	1.00	0.14	0.26	0.40	0.12	0.11	0.38	0.23	0.09	0.30	0.43	0.33	0.31	0.32
DE GLEs Gr.4 (2006)	0.14	1.00	0.09	0.16	0.13	0.11	0.17	0.19	0.11	0.16	0.17	0.19	0.15	0.16
ID Stnds Gr.4 (2006)	0.26	0.09	1.00	0.28	0.13	0.11	0.30	0.14	0.15	0.22	0.31	0.29	0.27	0.26
IN Stnds Gr.4 (2007)	0.40	0.16	0.28	1.00	0.14	0.18	0.38	0.17	0.19	0.48	0.34	0.42	0.35	0.30
KS Stnds Gr.4 (2005)	0.12	0.13	0.13	0.14	1.00	0.21	0.19	0.30	0.24	0.14	0.20	0.22	0.18	0.13
ME GLEs Gr.4 (2005)	0.11	0.11	0.11	0.18	0.21	1.00	0.14	0.19	0.23	0.18	0.16	0.18	0.17	0.11
MN ELAR Stnds. Gr.4 (2005)	0.38	0.17	0.30	0.38	0.19	0.14	1.00	0.28	0.18	0.33	0.45	0.42	0.42	0.30
MT R Stnds Gr.4 (2005)	0.23	0.19	0.14	0.17	0.30	0.19	0.28	1.00	0.19	0.19	0.25	0.25	0.22	0.22
NH Reading GLEs Gr.4 (2005)	0.09	0.11	0.15	0.19	0.24	0.23	0.18	0.19	1.00	0.13	0.12	0.18	0.17	0.13
OH Indctrs Gr.4 (2007)	0.30	0.16	0.22	0.48	0.14	0.18	0.33	0.19	0.13	1.00	0.29	0.39	0.31	0.30
OK Stnds Gr.4 (2005)	0.43	0.17	0.31	0.34	0.20	0.16	0.45	0.25	0.12	0.29	1.00	0.37	0.34	0.32
OR Stnds Gr.4 (2007)	0.33	0.19	0.29	0.42	0.22	0.18	0.42	0.25	0.18	0.39	0.37	1.00	0.39	0.28
VT GLEs Gr.4 (2006)	0.31	0.15	0.27	0.35	0.18	0.17	0.42	0.22	0.17	0.31	0.34	0.39	1.00	0.27
WI Stnds Gr.4 (2003)	0.32	0.16	0.26	0.30	0.13	0.11	0.30	0.22	0.13	0.30	0.32	0.28	0.27	1.00

	CA Stnds Gr.8	DE GLEs Gr.8	ID Stnds Gr.8	IN Stnds Gr.8	KS Stnds Gr.8	ME GLEs Gr.8	MN ELAR Stnds. Gr.8	MT R Stnds Gr.8	NH Reading GLEs Gr.8	OH Indctrs Gr.8	OK Stnds Gr.8	OR Stnds Gr.8	VT GLEs Gr.8	WI Stnds Gr.8
CA Stnds Gr.8 (2005)	1.00	0.28	0.31	0.35	0.39	0.12	0.46	0.22	0.21	0.47	0.13	0.43	0.39	0.38
DE GLEs Gr.8 (2005)	0.28	1.00	0.26	0.25	0.24	0.24	0.30	0.32	0.26	0.23	0.15	0.29	0.27	0.18
ID Stnds Gr.8 (2006)	0.31	0.26	1.00	0.29	0.31	0.13	0.34	0.13	0.18	0.32	0.11	0.40	0.31	0.26
IN Stnds Gr.8 (2006)	0.35	0.25	0.29	1.00	0.29	0.09	0.34	0.15	0.17	0.28	0.12	0.34	0.28	0.24
KS Stnds Gr.8 (2003)	0.39	0.24	0.31	0.29	1.00	0.16	0.37	0.24	0.24	0.38	0.15	0.38	0.39	0.24
ME GLEs Gr.8 (2005)	0.12	0.24	0.13	0.09	0.16	1.00	0.12	0.24	0.24	0.10	0.15	0.18	0.13	0.07
MN ELAR Stnds. Gr.8 (2005)	0.46	0.30	0.34	0.34	0.37	0.12	1.00	0.23	0.29	0.47	0.23	0.48	0.41	0.32
MT R Stnds Gr.8 (2005)	0.22	0.32	0.13	0.15	0.24	0.24	0.23	1.00	0.23	0.18	0.19	0.20	0.19	0.15
NH Reading GLEs Gr.8 (2005)	0.21	0.26	0.18	0.17	0.24	0.24	0.29	0.23	1.00	0.20	0.22	0.24	0.22	0.10
OH Indctrs Gr.8 (2005)	0.47	0.23	0.32	0.28	0.38	0.10	0.47	0.18	0.20	1.00	0.12	0.40	0.38	0.33
OK Stnds Gr.8 (2007)	0.13	0.15	0.11	0.12	0.15	0.15	0.23	0.19	0.22	0.12	1.00	0.19	0.18	0.08
OR Stnds Gr.8 (2007)	0.43	0.29	0.40	0.34	0.38	0.18	0.48	0.20	0.24	0.40	0.19	1.00	0.43	0.30
VT GLEs Gr.8 (2006)	0.39	0.27	0.31	0.28	0.39	0.13	0.41	0.19	0.22	0.38	0.18	0.43	1.00	0.22
WI Stnds Gr.8 (2003)	0.38	0.18	0.26	0.24	0.24	0.07	0.32	0.15	0.10	0.33	0.08	0.30	0.22	1.00

SOURCE: Porter, Polikoff, and Smithson (2008, Table 1).

This study, conducted jointly by the Fordham Foundation and the Northwest Evaluation Association (NWEA), was designed to address three questions:

1. Where are states setting the proficiency bar, and can their approaches to setting cut scores be compared in a fair way?
2. Given the pressure to bring 100 percent of students to proficient levels, are states lowering their standards over time in order to meet that goal?
3. Are cut scores relatively consistent in terms of difficulty level across grades?

Fordham and the NWEA decided to collaborate to conduct this study because the NWEA has developed a computer-adaptive assessment system that is used by many districts. The test is used primarily for diagnostic testing, so that districts can pinpoint the performance levels of individual students in different areas that are covered in the relevant state standards. Thus, the assessment is designed to be as well aligned as possible to the content standards of the states in which it is used. The NWEA maintains a large pool of items, and it constructs tests for districts by using the items that are closest to the standards for which that district is responsible. Because all the items are pegged to a common scale, the NWEA is able to make some comparisons across states.

With this resource, the researchers were able to estimate where on the NWEA scale a given state is setting its cut score. In many cases, that calculation was available for two times, 2003 and 2006, and thus they were able to consider the possibility that the cut scores had changed over time in those states. They had data for a total of 830,000 students in 26 states who had taken both the NWEA assessment and their own state exam.

The researchers' primary finding was that there is enormous variability in the level of difficulty of states' tests—a range from approximately the 6th percentile (94 percent would pass) to approximately the 77th percentile (23 percent would pass). These findings are shown in Figure 2-3.

To illustrate the kinds of differences these numbers represent, Petrilli provided two sample grade 4 items from the NWEA assessment, each with a difficulty level at the cut score of one of the states. For the Wisconsin cut score, which they had calculated at the 16th percentile on the NWEA scale, the sample item asked students to select from a group of sentences the one that "tells a fact, not an opinion." To represent the comparable cut score for Massachusetts, calculated at the 65th percentile, Petrilli showed an item that asked students to read a complex, difficult passage (excerpted from a work by Leo Tolstoy) and to pick from a list of factual statements the one that is actually found in the passage.

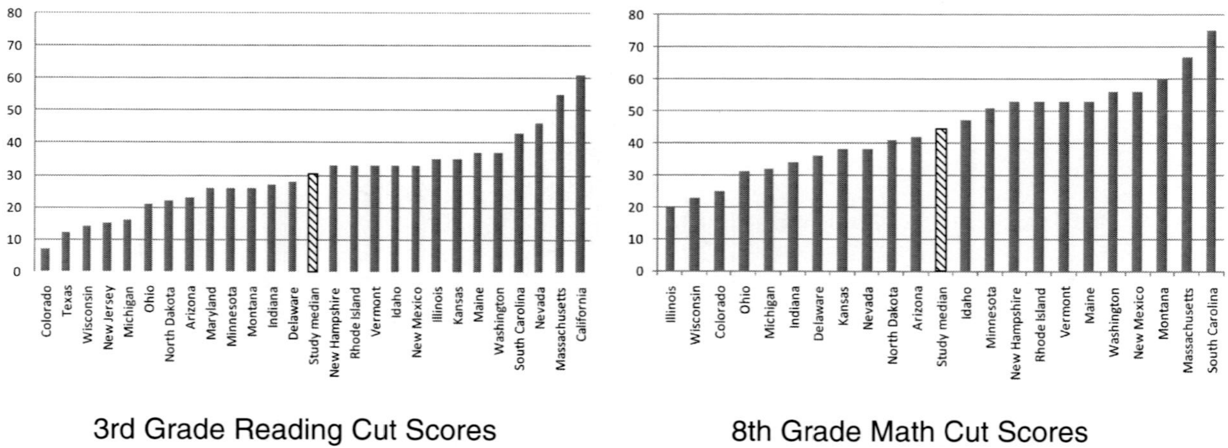

FIGURE 2-3 Difference in difficulty of state tests.
SOURCE: Petrilli (2008).

Petrilli believes the implications of this degree of difference are profound. If, as many people believe, the high stakes attached to state tests mean that teachers focus the bulk of their attention on the students who are just below the proficient level, to get them over that bar, then teachers in Wisconsin will be targeting their instruction at a very low level in comparison to those in Massachusetts. This analytical approach also made it possible to compare the cut scores that states set for mathematics and for reading, at least in terms of percentiles. Doing so is useful, Petrilli explained, because test results that seem to demonstrate that students are doing better in one subject than another, may actually demonstrate that the level of mastery needed to score at the proficient level is quite different for each subject.

With regard to the second question, whether states are engaged in a so-called race to the bottom, the researchers were surprised to find that this does not seem to be the case. Rather, Petrilli characterized the trend as a "walk to the middle." Most states kept their cut scores relatively consistent across the time period studied, but the states that began with the highest standards had moderated their standards somewhat, while those with the lowest standards had raised theirs. He cautioned, however, that because they were working with percentiles, the change over time could be explained either by intentional shifts in cut scores or by changes in students' actual achievement levels.

In terms of the last question, the vertical alignment of state standards, the analysis showed that they are not well calibrated, grade level to grade level. In the majority of states, the elementary standards are set significantly lower than the middle school standards. When this is the case, students may have no trouble with the grade 3 test, proceed normally through subsequent grades, and then stumble on the grade 8 test. The aggregate results may inaccurately indicate a problem with middle school instruction, in comparison to elementary school instruction. Moreover, if standards are not aligned vertically, the test results will not be good indicators of students' growth over time.

Petrilli drew three conclusions from the research. First, state performance standards need "an overhaul." If the goal is for standards to progress cumulatively from kindergarten through grade 12, states should begin with rigorous high school graduation requirements and work backward to develop vertically aligned standards. Second, Petrilli believes that the objective of bringing 100 percent of students to proficiency has become a perverse incentive that has the effect of lowering achievement. Finally, in responding to the workshop theme, he said that discussion of national standards should continue—that such discussion would have the effect of creating consistent objectives for students across the states.

Performance Standards

Another way to examine the question of how much performance expectations vary across states is to use the National Assessment of Educational Progress (NAEP). NCLB requires not only that states report progress on their own assessments, but also that they participate in NAEP so that it can serve as a common yardstick for comparing students' proficiency across states. The results of these comparisons indicate striking discrepancies between the performance required for proficiency on state assessments and what is required for proficiency on NAEP assessments. These results have received significant public attention, and, as presenter Peggy Carr explained, the National Center for Education Statistics (NCES) recognized the need for a more precise methodology with which to make these comparisons (see National Center for Education Statistics, 2007).

Figure 2-4 illustrates the discrepancies between the proficiency levels that states use to report their adequate yearly progress and the NAEP proficiency levels, in terms of percentages of students meeting the standard.

This information is useful to provide a snapshot, Carr explained. Since each state is asked to use NAEP as a benchmark, the comparison between each state and NAEP is valid. However, comparing states just by using the percentage meeting the standard is less useful. Consequently,

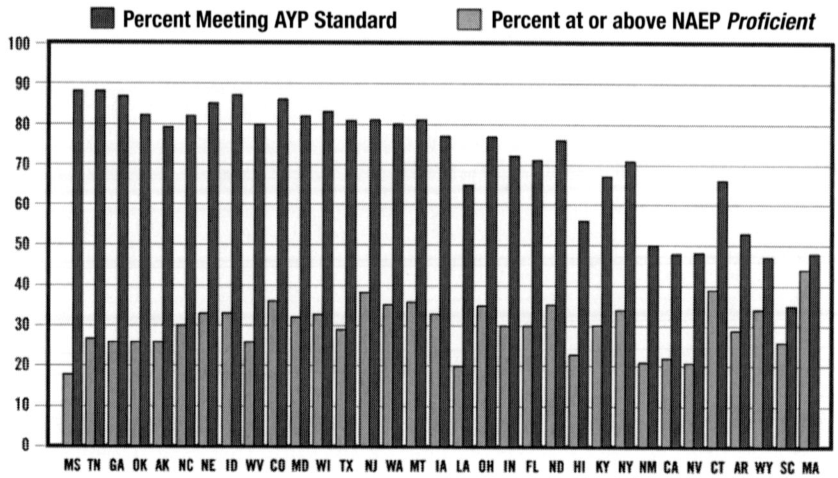

FIGURE 2-4 A comparison of state proficiency and NAEP standards.
SOURCE: Carr (2008).

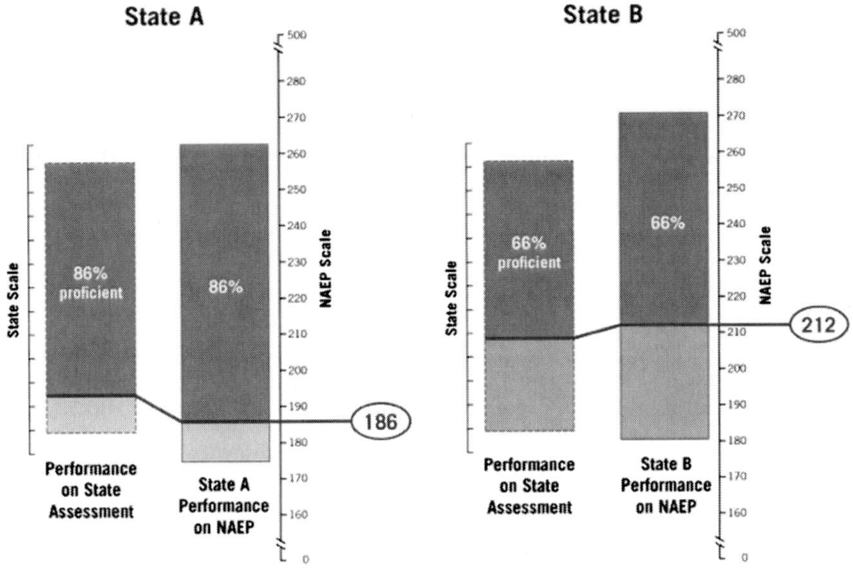

FIGURE 2-5 Methodology for comparing state proficiency standards.
SOURCE: Carr (2008).

NCES staff used an equipercentile equating method to align the distributions of pairs of scales, the NAEP scale and that of each of the states. In other words, they used results from schools that had participated in NAEP to calculate what they called a NAEP-equivalent score on the state assessment. Having done that for each state, they could then compare the NAEP-equivalent scores of any state with that of any other. What the comparison shows is the relative degree of challenge of a state's standards using the NAEP scale as the common yardstick. Figure 2-5 shows how the comparison works for two hypothetical states.

The results of this analysis were quite similar to the results of the Fordham/NWEA analysis. Generally, the researchers found that states' proficiency levels varied significantly and that the majority map onto the "below basic" range on the NAEP scale, although the distribution varied by subject and grade. The results for mathematics are shown in Figures 2-6 and 2-7.

The researchers also looked at the correlation between the proportion of students that a state reports as meeting its proficiency standards and the NAEP-equivalent score. They found that the correlation was negative: that is, the higher the number of students that a state reports are passing its own standards, the less challenging are that state's standards. The researchers also found that the position of a state's adequate yearly

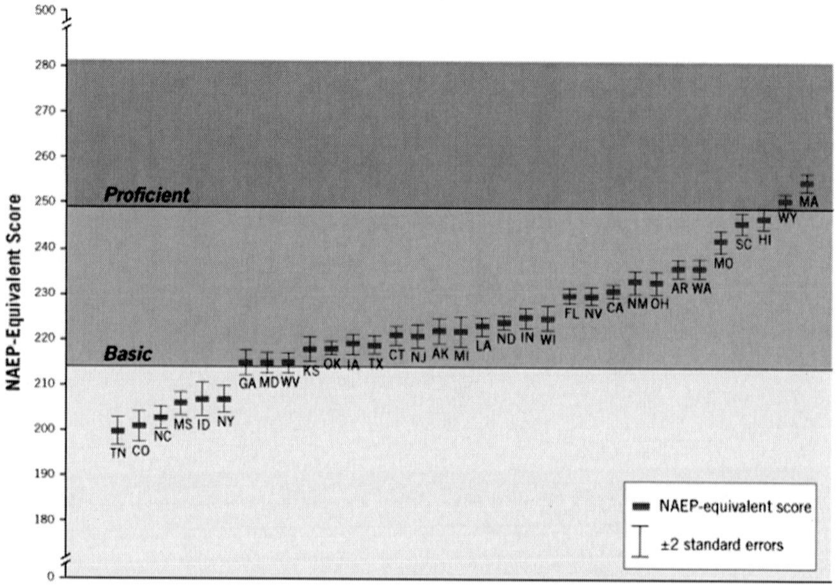

FIGURE 2-6 A comparison of proficiency standards in grade 4 mathematics.
SOURCE: Carr (2008).

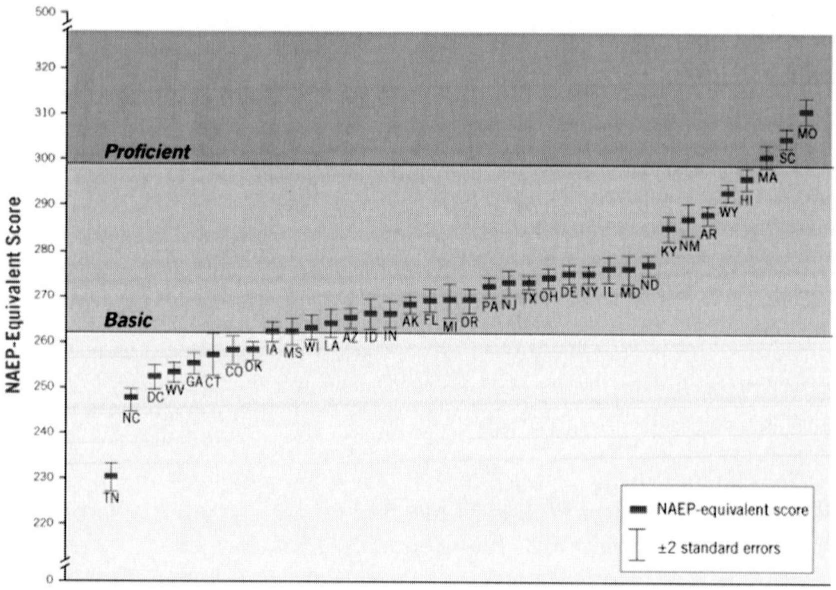

FIGURE 2-7 A comparison of proficiency standards in grade 8 mathematics.
SOURCE: Carr (2008).

progress standards on the NAEP scale bears little relationship to that state's performance on the NAEP assessment. In other words, students' performance on NAEP cannot be predicted from the relative difficulty of the state's own standards.

Carr's conclusions from these results were similar to Petrilli's. To illustrate their significance, she highlighted the results for three contiguous states, Georgia, North Carolina, and South Carolina. Students in these three states all perform at about the same level on the NAEP reading assessment, but the states have set very different standards for their students. An example of the practical effect of this discrepancy is that a student who moves from North Carolina to South Carolina might go from being viewed as a proficient reader to being placed in a remedial class. Her closing point was that state assessments vary widely in both content and design, and that states may attach different meanings to the label "proficient." In the context of NAEP, proficiency is defined as "competency over challenging subject matter," whereas states generally define proficiency as grade-level performance.

Participants and discussants had a range of comments about the variation that was described, factors that may contribute to it, and its implications. Discussant Barbara Reys drew on her experiences co-chairing the standards development process for mathematics in Missouri to highlight some of the practical challenges of working toward common standards. Apart from the requirements of states that prize their autonomy, she noted the limitations of existing national standards, which may not be grade specific and lack other critical details. She was not surprised at the finding that many states' standards do not align with national ones because "it's really the decisions about what you want to focus on at particular grades that are the tough ones."

Reys also showed some results from an analysis of consistency she had conducted of K-8 mathematics standards. Her findings echoed those already presented. She found dramatic variation from state to state in the grade placement of particular concepts. The critical finding was again that a given learning expectation might be found in the grade 1 standards in one state and in the grade 3 standards in another state.

These differences create a significant complication for textbook publishers who want to serve multiples states. From Reys's analysis, only 4 of 108 possible learning expectations for fourth graders were common across 10 states—suggesting that a textbook publisher might choose to incorporate all 108 of them. Since the content of textbooks has a significant effect on teachers' instructional plans, this lack of overlap becomes a self-reinforcing pressure against curricular focus. At the same time, however, textbooks are a potential tool for increasing uniformity because they are so influential.

Discussant William Schmidt characterized the variation among state standards as "enormous." He believes that both mathematics and science standards display "the maximum possible variation at every combination of grade level and topic." He suggested that this is particularly bad for mathematics because that subject has an inherent logic, so that it is essential that students learn concepts in a particular order if they are to develop sound mathematical thinking. The problem, he said, is that because so few standards establish coherence and vertical alignment in mathematics goals, the result is a mishmash, with many concepts being introduced far too early and then repeated over and over in subsequent grades. Ironically, he explained, the topics that get the least coverage tend to be the most important—the deeper topics that build conceptual understanding.

Schmidt has also observed that district standards vary as much as those of states. Moreover, he suggested, variation at the classroom level, in terms of what teachers are actually covering with their students, far outpaces the variation at the district and state levels. For Schmidt, this variation, which permeates the entire education system, is "the Achilles heel of the No Child Left Behind Act." Based on his analysis, he argued that the degree of variation in the opportunities children have to learn makes it inevitable that many will be left behind.

Discussant Peter McWalters offered a perspective from Rhode Island, which has coordinated its standards development with two other states, New Hampshire and Vermont.[3] Although the presentation suggested a number of questions for this consortium of states to ponder as they work to improve their standards, he labeled the effort a success and added that he would be happy to see a national model. He noted that NCLB had been the impetus for the efforts of the New England states because none of the three has a testing infrastructure and all are too small to produce what is required on their own. They were also fortunate in that none of them has regulatory requirements, such as state-mandated standards, that would present a barrier to the states working collectively.

However, McWalters identified what he sees a major stumbling block to a national approach to standards—that "no state would trust the feds after our experience with the beginning of No Child Left Behind. . . . There is zero trust." He also supported points made earlier regarding states' capacity to change in the ways that are needed. For him, the biggest challenge is to find ways to serve diverse students with diverse needs. To do that successfully, teachers will need a command of their subjects—the content and the pedagogy that is "way beyond what we currently have."

[3]The three-state consortium, the New England Common Assessment Program, is discussed in greater detail in Chapter 7.

PARADOXES

Committee chair Lorraine McDonnell reflected that the discussion of standards as they are currently operating, and the findings regarding variation across the states, yielded two significant paradoxes. The first is that, although standards are very well institutionalized across the country, with very few voices challenging their value as an organizing framework for reform, it is also the case that standards-based reform means different things to different people. The term in some ways disguises deep-seated differences about both priorities and strategies for achieving education goals.

The second paradox is that, although there is little ostensible disagreement about the standards-based approach, there is a wide gap between the theoretical model and the reality of standards-based accountability systems in practice. The theoretical model of an aligned system is compelling as a strategy for meeting the needs of diverse students. Yet in practice, states and districts have lacked the capacity, resources, and, perhaps in some cases, the knowledge or the will to put all the essential elements into place. Participants described legislators and other policy makers who have viewed the development of a new core curriculum or the raising of high school graduation standards as all that is required to pursue standards-based reform. Disputes over the significance of testing results, and the effects the reporting of these results can have, have further clouded the discussion.

The result is a situation in which the core concept—the goal of defining standards and holding educators accountable for the results—seems to be constant across states, but in which the execution of this goal yields starkly different results.

3

Considering the Options

The descriptive picture of standards as they are currently operating provided important background for the discussion, but in order to examine the pros and cons of a move to common standards, the committee wanted also to consider the relative merits of specific aspects of states' approaches. The terms "standards" and "standards-based reform" are loosely used to refer to complex sets of policies, practices, and documents that states use to define performance expectations, and it seems fair to say that each state has devised a unique variation on this theme. While the existence of so many distinct approaches may present problems, a persuasive case might be made for the superiority of any one of them. Devising a set of common standards would entail making a series of choices among competing approaches. Fundamental to that task would be a way to understand the primary characteristics that distinguish one approach from another, as well as a way of evaluating the pros and cons of competing options.

The committee developed a two-part framework for keeping track of the many moving parts in an analysis of options for common standards. The first part addresses the primary options or policy choices; the second part addresses criteria for evaluating the options. The primary policy choices to be made include:

- identifying a process for agreeing on common standards;
- determining the intended scope of the standards across subjects, grades, and states; and
- determining how the standards will be implemented.

The committee developed the graphic representation of these choice points shown in Figure 3-1. The graphic is structured to emphasize that possibilities in each of these areas exist along a continuum, and that in practice the categories might be blended in innovative ways.

Any number of factors might also influence decisions about the development process, the scope, and the implementation, but most are likely to be subsumed under four primary categories: quality, equity, feasibility, and opportunity cost. The committee therefore developed a second component to the framework to guide discussion of how one might evaluate competing approaches to common standards, shown in Table 3-1.

The framework was intended simply as a guide to discussion, to ensure that key elements were not overlooked. Participants referred back to it frequently but also pointed out several elements that it does not take into account. The forward momentum of institutions that are already in place is one factor that is not addressed—particularly the assessment and accountability structures at the state and federal levels, which are likely to have a powerful influence over any changes that could be made to standards. As one participant put it, "the standards conversation could get trapped by the problem of how and what you measure—so that has to be on the table from the start." Another pointed out that policy change rarely takes place according to logical frameworks, and that a bottom-up push, perhaps stimulated by the examples set by independent groups, such as the advanced placement or international baccalaureate programs, could end up influencing the outcome significantly.

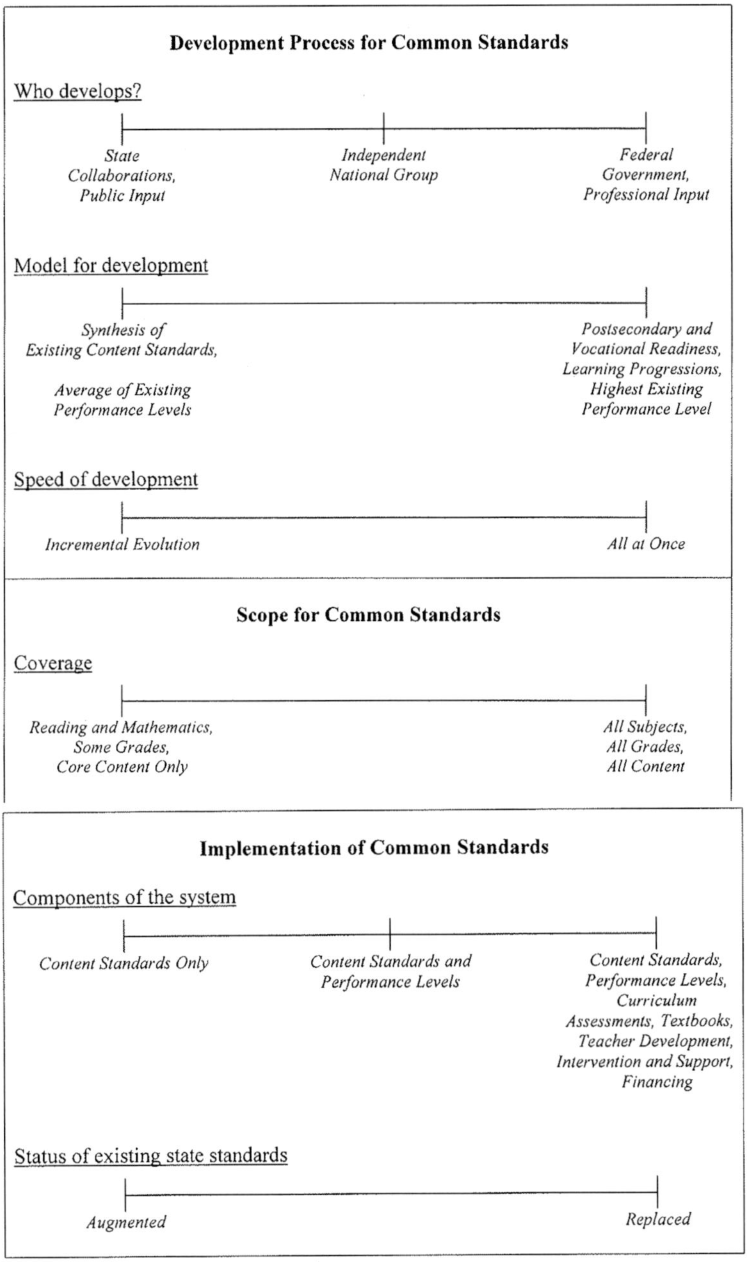

FIGURE 3-1 Draft options framework.

TABLE 3-1 Evaluation Framework

Quality	• Effects on the quality of the standards themselves, such as their clarity, comprehensiveness, and developmental appropriateness. • Effects on the quality of other components of the education system, such as assessments, curriculum, textbooks/materials, the accountability system, and the teacher workforce. • Effects on outcomes, such as student achievement and graduation rates.
Equity	• Effects on expectations for student learning, as embodied in content and performance standards. • Effects on equity of components of the education system, as reflected in funding, teachers, placement, opportunity to learn, other factors. • Effects on outcomes, such as achievement gap, differential dropout rates.
Feasibility	• Political feasibility of moving toward common standards. • Cost of moving toward common standards. • Capacity requirements to move toward common standards.
Opportunity cost	Evaluation of what might be lost if policy attention focuses on common standards at the expense of alternative policy options, such as improving No Child Left Behind, improving teacher preparation, etc.

4

Analyzing Quality and Impact

With the options and evaluation framework as a general guide, the workshop discussion turned to specific analyses that could be used in evaluating aspects of standards and standards-based reform.

QUALITY OF CONTENT STANDARDS

Perhaps most straightforward have been questions about the quality of content standards themselves, but even this kind of analysis is more complicated than it might seem. Karen Wixson presented an overview of the rating schemes that have been used by four national organizations—Achieve, Inc., the American Federation of Teachers, *Education Week*, the and Fordham Foundation—to evaluate the quality of state content standards. She found that, overall, the groups each included some, but not all, of the following evaluation criteria:

- Specificity,
- Clarity,
- Subject and grade coverage,
- Coverage of subject-specific topics,
- Rigor/demand of topics,
- Balance of knowledge and skills,
- Teaching approaches, and
- Policy and practice changes to implement standards.

None of the groups considered all of these criteria, and even when they

TABLE 4-1 Examples of Evaluation Criteria Related to Standards Content

Achieve, Inc.	Important subject matter—require use and application of agreed-on core subject matter.
American Federation of Teachers	Should include the following particular content: • In reading should cover reading basics (e.g., word attack, skills, vocabulary) and reading comprehension (e.g., exposure to a variety of literary genres). • In mathematics should cover number sense and operations, measurement, geometry, data analysis and probability, and algebra and functions. Should give attention to both content and skills.
Education Week	Should cover the core subjects of English, mathematics, science, and history/social studies.
Fordham Foundation	• Inclusion of particular content. • Avoiding influence of 1990s-era national standards. • Rigor of content. • Adequate attention to content knowledge versus skills.

SOURCE: Committee compilation of criteria used in reports by the organizations listed.

seem to identify the same criteria, they do not necessarily use the terms in the same way.

Looking just at content, for example, Wixson demonstrated the range of perspectives. Table 4-1 shows the language related to content used by each group. Although each group's text is best understood in the context of its overall presentation of its evaluation criteria, important differences are evident.

Wixson also noted that a critical element was missing from the criteria described by all the groups: the perspectives of experts from the academic disciplines. Discipline experts are often involved when standards are developed, and many such groups have produced cogent descriptions of the ways learning develops within academic disciplines, as well as of the key concepts in each discipline that students need to master as they progress.[1] Drawing on research on learning and cognition as well as on content expertise, these descriptions emphasize the integration of learning and understanding and the ways that factual learning, conceptual

[1]Research in mathematics and science education, in particular, has yielded advances in the understanding of how students learn complex content and of the corresponding "content pedagogy"—that is, understanding of complex content integrated with understanding of how best to teach it—that teachers need (see National Research Council, 2001, 2006).

understanding, and developing skills reinforce one another throughout the K-12 learning progression they are describing (see National Research Council, 2000).

These more complex views of learning, however, are often overlooked in the context of assessment and accountability programs. Discrete skills and factual knowledge are relatively easy to assess, while the aspects of learning that discipline experts describe, such as developing conceptual understanding or the capacity to retrieve and apply factual knowledge to solve problems, are not. The consequence, in Wixson's view, is that the development process tends to winnow out the more complex and nuanced elements of learning in a discipline, and that the resulting state content standards are significantly curtailed versions of what discipline experts have described. She believes that the No Child Left Behind (NCLB) assessment requirements have exacerbated this problem—an unintended negative consequence of a program that was intended to move states away from the low-level basic skills standards that many of them used in the 1970s and 1980s.

The impact of these comparatively meager content standards is far-reaching. Without the discipline-based perspective, the focus tends to be on static, linear development of knowledge, rather than on developmentally appropriate learning progressions. Teachers must have what is called pedagogical content knowledge, and this has been defined for various fields, in order to foster this kind of learning in their students, but the importance of this preparation is easily overlooked if the learning progressions are not described in the state standards. In practice, Wixson observed, it is the standards for elementary and middle school students that are the least likely to reflect more sophisticated conceptions of learning in the disciplines, yet students will need that type of preparation in order to succeed with the challenging coursework encouraged in high school by many states, such as the advanced placement or international baccalaureate programs.

Some participants suggested that the significant problem is not so much the way that content standards frame expectations for students at each level, but rather that assessments have come to be the de facto standards. As one put it, "whatever gets on the test is what gets taught," and thus the deciding factor tends to be whether or not a learning objective can be assessed using a multiple-choice question. Others pointed out that standards that specify grade-by-grade expectations for students are critical guides for instruction, but that discipline experts may not be in a position to support firm recommendations about when particular elements should be introduced. While most people would agree that the content standards should be both logical and coherent, the many practical purposes for which standards are needed may not all be met by the descriptions provided by discipline experts.

IMPACT OF STANDARDS ON TEACHING AND LEARNING

Examining the extent of variation across the states was relatively straightforward. The evidence seems clearly to suggest that the current arrangement, in which each state devises its own content and performance standards, is characterized by dramatic variation in what and how much students are asked to learn. This information does not directly answer, however, the broader questions of what real impact that variation has had on teaching and learning, and what benefits a set of common standards that was widely adopted might bring. Douglas Harris explored possible ways to investigate these questions empirically.[2] He began by considering the possibility that common standards might have the effect of improving education by:

- providing better instructional coordination across schools and grade levels;
- allowing students to experience higher level academic content;
- addressing inequities, since disadvantaged students are more likely to be offered lower level content;
- providing concrete, more conceptually based guidance to teachers; and
- improving fairness and the effectiveness of federal and state accountability.

In theory, any set of standards (not just standards common to all states) might have these effects, so Harris considered the kinds of evidence that might indicate whether existing standards have solved these problems. His conclusion is that the most apparently promising evidence actually reveals relatively little about the impact of standards on teaching and learning. For example, the dramatic variety in performance expectations, textbook coverage, and enacted curricula seems to reflect an unequal distribution of high-quality instruction. However, this variety is the result of decentralization and local experimentation, which, Harris asserted, "many see as the system's greatest strength." Similarly, the marked overlap in topic coverage across grades may mean dull repetition in many cases, but it is partly deliberate and may also have advantages—the analyses may

[2]Harris also developed a paper on this topic, which is available at http://www7.nationalacademies.org/cfe/State_Standards_Workshop_1_Agenda.html [May 2008].

not be able to capture iterations in the instruction on a particular topic that promote growth in students' conceptual thinking, for example.

Other possible evidence includes findings from international research that highly centralized education systems are associated with higher aggregate achievements, and that schools with high achievement results tend to be those with high academic expectations. These findings also provide limited support for inferences about the effects of standards themselves, because they offer correlations, but not causal evidence.

What then, might provide stronger evidence? Ideally, Harris explained, one would randomly assign entire states to treatment and control groups, measure student outcomes, and then wait patiently to observe possible systemic effects. Since this method is not possible, a feasible alternative might be to conduct quasi-experimental analyses of the relationship between standards and student outcomes, by observing what happens when states make specific changes in their policies. Harris speculated, however, that this method would demonstrate no clear effects because standards have relatively minor influence by themselves. In changing its standards, a state is making "a small reform. You are not putting tons of resources in. You are not changing who is in the classroom. You are not changing what teachers know. You are not changing a lot of what's going on in the classroom, at least in an immediate sense." And, of course, any change that might result would take years, which is a further complication, because many other factors might change markedly over the period in which one might expect to see standards have an impact—thus blurring the effects of the standards themselves.

Even if the ideal research methods are of limited utility in studying the effects of this type of policy change, Harris argued, "we can't just throw up our hands and say we can't understand this. . . . That always gives the benefit of the doubt to the status quo." There are other options. One would be to review the effects of standards on intermediate outcomes, such as instruction and the enacted curriculum, teacher preparation, professional development, textbook design and adoption, or changes in the way schools are administered. Finding out, for example, whether teachers are aware of the specifics of revised standards and report that they attempt to apply them, or whether changes in textbook content or teacher professional development align with revised standards, would reveal important effects (or noneffects).

Another strategy would be to use quasi-experimental techniques, such as value-added modeling, to look at changes in student outcomes in the context of changes in standards or changes in enacted curricula. Another possibility would be to find schools in which changes in standards have apparently had an influence and do "reverse engineering" by examining the apparent mechanisms for change and comparing the circumstances in that setting with those in a school that did not seem to change.

While it is important to investigate the impact of standards, Harris observed, he was mindful that standards are intended to serve as the nucleus of the network of linked elements of an aligned education system: curriculum, instruction, assessment, teacher preparation and professional development, etc. It would be unreasonable to expect that simply establishing standards would be sufficient to bring about improvement in teaching and learning, so looking for effects without considering the other elements would be missing the point. And the most influential of the related elements of the system in practice is surely the accountability system. That is, schools tend to pay most attention to standards that are assessed, so the effects of standards might be most evident in studies of accountability systems. Harris suggested that refining the research question about standards, so that one considers them as variables that moderate the effects of accountability on students outcomes, might be a more useful kind of analysis then a search for the impact of standards themselves.

Harris also noted that it is important to consider possible negative impacts as well. For example, it is possible that the reduction in flexibility that may come with new standards could discourage teachers who are already effective, or it could discourage desirable prospective teachers. His primary message was that the understanding of the effects of standards needed to support sound policy decisions must be pieced together from imperfect sources of evidence—and that empirical evidence alone may not be sufficient to answer the policy question of what benefits common standards might bring.

Laurie Wise provided another perspective on analysis of the impact of standards on achievement, which followed up on the findings from the National Assessment of Educational Progress (NAEP) analysis described earlier by Peggy Carr (National Center for Education Statistics, 2007). That study showed that states vary widely in where they set their proficiency-level cut scores—some have very high expectations for students, and some have very low ones. The question is, does it matter? One way to approach this question is to examine whether states that have set high proficiency standards subsequently showed greater improvement in student achievement scores on NAEP. If one assumes, Wise explained, that content differences matter less than differences in performance expectations (because if the standard is set high, the necessary resources will be marshaled to meet it), then the achievement scores should rise with higher proficiency standards. He looked for that relationship across two periods, 2003 to 2005 and 2005 to 2007.

Wise started with the results of the National Center for Education

Statistics study, which provided a way of comparing the proficiency scales used in individual states with the NAEP scales, and confirmed the wide range of state proficiency standards. By comparison, however, students' performance on NAEP varies much less by state than the dramatically different state proficiency cut scores would suggest. Wise found a modest correlation between the percentage of students who were proficient on the state's assessment and their performance on NAEP, but he also found that "if a state had a high percent of students scoring at the proficient level, it's almost sure that they set a very low cut point."

The bottom line, however, was that Wise found no statistically significant relationship between states' proficiency cut scores and their students' gains on NAEP across the two periods he examined. His initial conclusion was that other factors, such as coherent content standards and the quality of curriculum and instruction, may be more important than where the proficiency cut scores are set. He suggested that more careful study is needed, perhaps along the lines Harris suggested, to explore the full chain of causal factors that have impact on student achievement.

5

Costs

While saving money is not the primary goal cited by most advocates of common standards, questions about what it costs states to have standards and how those costs might be affected by a switch to common standards are nevertheless important. These questions raise a host of complexities. Calculating the cost of a policy that can be implemented in a seemingly infinite number of ways is a formidable challenge in itself, but economists also consider what they refer to as opportunity costs—the value of the potential benefits of policy options not chosen—when they evaluate the costs of different choices.

Looking first at the question of what states must spend in order to have standards, the committee identified five framing questions to guide the discussion:

1. What are the major activities states undertake to develop and maintain a standards-based K-12 education system? What is the nature of the costs to states associated with each of these major activities?
2. What are the sources of variation in these costs by state?
3. What are the costs associated with each major activity across select states?
4. How much do state cost estimates vary for each activity?
5. What are the conceptual and technical issues involved in developing empirical estimates of these costs?

Margaret Goertz presented a framework for considering the costs, providing an analysis of what states actually do in implementing a standards-based K-12 education system (Goertz, 2008). Douglas Harris and Lori Taylor followed with a detailed investigation of the challenges of estimating the costs of this kind of enterprise, as well as empirical estimates of the costs incurred in three states: Florida, North Dakota, and Texas (Harris and Taylor, 2008b).

COST ESTIMATION FRAMEWORK

Goertz organized her framework around what she identified as the six primary activities that constitute a standards-based reform system, although she noted that others might define the major activities differently (see Box 5-1). Goertz cautioned that the first four activities, which describe the mechanics of the standards themselves and the accountability system, generally receive most of the attention, but that the last two activities, which describe the ways in which the standards and accountability system may affect teaching and learning, are equally important.

Goertz used these six activities as the basis for a discussion of ways in which variation in implementation may affect the costs to states. Looking at the first three activities, she identified several primary sources of variation with cost implications. The frequency with which a state reviews and revises its standards and updates its assessments (as well as the number of subjects for which there are standards and the number of assessments) is one factor. A second factor is the process used for setting and reviewing content and performance standards, which varies in complexity, in part because of the number of people and groups involved. States may rely primarily on their department of education staff and volunteers, for example, or hire a contractor, use paid experts, or perhaps do all three.

With regard to rewards and sanctions (activity 4), there is a large range of approaches and of potential costs. Reponses to classifications of schools or districts as falling short of No Child Left Behind (NCLB) performance targets might begin with instructional audits or needs assessments. Interventions might include developing school improvement plans, measures to build capacity at the district level, or professional development in such areas as curriculum and instruction, data analysis, assessment, and leadership. For failing students, states vary in terms of how they determine eligibility and in how they structure and deliver remediation, as well as in how much funding may be available from the state for this purpose.

The characteristics of a state also play a significant role. Readily apparent differences, such as the size of a state and the demographics of its student population, affect costs in predictable ways, but other factors are important as well. States vary in their mechanisms for funding

BOX 5-1
Major Standards-Based Reform Activities

1. Standards-setting

- Developing and revising academic content standards
- Setting performance standards
- Disseminating standards and training

2. State Assessment

- Aligning assessment with standards
- Item development
- Test construction
- Test administration
- Test scoring
- Score reporting
- Technical review, validation of the system

3. State Accountability System

- Data system (student, school, district)
- Reporting (school, district)
- Identifying school status, monitoring progress
- Other accountability measures (process, etc.)

4. Rewards and Sanctions

- Rewards to successful/improving schools
- Sanctions for underperforming/failing districts, schools, or students
- Intervention for failing schools, districts
- Intervention for failing students

5. Alignment with Other Policies

- Teacher preparation and program approval
- Teacher certification and licensure
- Curriculum (also textbook adoption in some states)

6. Instruction Delivery System

- Supporting teachers, schools, and districts in implementing new or revised standards (professional development, curriculum alignment, resources for expanded standards, adequacy studies to determine what would be required to give all students the opportunity to meet proficiency standards)
- Supporting students in meeting more challenging standards (programs and resources to address special education needs)

SOURCE: Goertz (2008).

public education and in the relative share that is paid by districts. States that have had standards-based reform policies for a decade or more are likely to have more firmly established systems and streamlined processes, which reduce costs. States with newer policies may thus have somewhat higher costs. A state's fiscal health also plays a role, perhaps because education budgets may remain more stable in the absence of economic downturns.

A key component of the variation in costs is the number of person hours required to accomplish the tasks involved. Salaries for regular staff, fees for consultants or contractors, and stipends for teachers who take on extra responsibilities are the prime costs for most of the activities. States also incur meeting and travel costs, as well as the costs of providing grants to districts, schools, or regional consortia. These are all costs that can be estimated, but Goertz noted that it is inherently more difficult to estimate the cost of a policy idea, such as standards-based reform, than a specific program.

Goertz returned to a point raised earlier, that standards-based reform is a term that can mean different things to different people. In order to estimate costs, one must determine which expenditures should be classed as standards-based reform costs and which are general K-12 education costs. One must also ask which costs would be incurred by states even without that conceptual approach and which are extra expenditures. Another complication is the task of distinguishing state costs from local costs. Since state education funding formulas vary, the extent to which costs incurred at the local level are covered by state K-12 education funding can vary significantly—which makes it more difficult to compare across states.

APPLYING THE FRAMEWORK IN THREE STATES

Harris and Taylor echoed the points that standards-based reform is a complex idea and that developing cost estimates for an idea is inherently difficult. Thus, in their analysis of the costs, they focused on three questions:

1. What costs are now being incurred to create, update, and minimally comply with current state and federal laws and rules regarding standards, assessments, and accountability?
2. What costs would the nation incur if the state-based system of standards, assessments, and accountability required by NCLB were implemented as a common system?
3. What are the costs of some of the specific "add-ons" to these systems that are not required by state or federal law?

To answer these questions, they first developed estimates of the costs of standards-based reform activities for three states—Florida, North Dakota, and Texas—that were chosen to reflect a range in terms of size, education spending, and approaches to assessment and accountability.[1] Their notion was that, since no one state could be viewed as representative or typical, they could use the data from these three states to compile a cost profile for a "typical state" and use that to calculate costs for the nation. They noted that their estimates are all based on the costs of simply complying with all requirements, rather than the costs of meeting goals, such as bringing all students to proficiency.

The challenge of comparing the costs of the current system with those of a potential common system raises several economic concepts. One important distinction is that between fixed costs, which are the same regardless of the scale of the program, and variable costs, which vary depending on the scale of the effort. A significant fixed cost of standards-based reform is developing the content standards and setting the performance standards: this cost would be the same whether the standards were to apply to 100 or 1 million students. However, Harris explained, a common standard is likely to set a higher bar, which is likely to mean significant additional costs. Moreover, a substantial majority of the costs of standards-based reform are variable and depend on design decisions (including how high the bar is set). Other variables would be the number of subjects and grade levels to be included, the frequency of assessment, the degree of support provided to schools, and the incentives and sanctions to be implemented.

Another distinction used by economists is that between opportunity costs and expenditures: reforms may switch resources from one activity to another, and it is important to include such resource costs in the cost estimate, even if they do not result in new expenditures. So, for example, the time that teachers need to spend on testing-related tasks does not require additional state or district expenditures because the teachers would otherwise have been engaged in another task and would be receiving their salaries. However, there is a real resource cost in the loss of whatever they might otherwise have accomplished during that time. Harris and Taylor focused on these costs (they used the term "real resource costs" to avoid technical jargon) in order to capture that value.

Harris and Taylor highlighted some of the features of the three states' systems to illustrate more specifically the kinds of variation that affect costs. For example, Florida and Texas have both gone consider-

[1]Harris and Taylor conferred with committee members in finalizing the list of states for analysis so that their results could be considered together with those of Massell's study discussed in Chapter 1.

ably beyond NCLB requirements (by testing at more grades and in more subjects), whereas North Dakota has not. Florida has a bonus program so that districts can give substantial monetary rewards to teachers for improvements made by their students, and Texas has a program to identify and accelerate certain students. Assigning the costs of these kinds of policies is complex, Harris explained, because one could argue that they are part of the cost of meeting the requirement—to push students toward proficiency—or one could argue that they are not required elements of a standards-based reform system. Moreover, a state government might reallocate resources in a way that poses a conundrum for cost estimators, for example, by switching instruction time from music to mathematics. If making this change is not treated as a cost, the implication is that music instruction has no value. Assigning a dollar value to what is lost is not straightforward, but treating it as an additional cost may unreasonably inflate the overall estimate.

Having described some of the issues and assumptions that guided their work, Harris and Taylor presented their cost data (their paper provides further detail about the costs they considered; see Harris and Taylor, 2008b). Their principal sources were national databases, data made publicly available by the three states, and interviews with local officials. Looking first at the costs per pupil and per standard (e.g., grade 3 mathematics) of developing standards, the authors included both per-pupil and per-standard costs in order to capture both one-time (initial development) and annual costs (such as those for administering assessments). Those results are shown in Table 5-1.

Harris and Taylor also calculated the overall costs per student of assessment and accountability programs in each state, shown in Table 5-2, and some of the additional fixed costs states incur when they go beyond legal requirements, in this case the cost of annual reviews of the standards. These figures are shown in Table 5-3. For context, annual expenditures

TABLE 5-1 Estimated Cost of Developing Academic Standards in Three States

State	Cost per Subject and Grade Level Standard
Florida	$45,000
North Dakota	$18,000
Texas	$32,000

SOURCE: Harris and Taylor (2008a).

TABLE 5-2 Estimated Costs of Assessment and Accountability Per Student

	Florida	North Dakota	Texas
State			
Test contracts	$15	$34	$20
Other assessment	$10	$10	$3
Accountability	$8	$1	$1
Local			
Test administration	$35	$24	$24
Professional development	$53	$64	$65
Data management	$15	$6	$11
Total	$136	$139	$123

NOTE: Estimates are the lower bound estimates for real resource costs.
SOURCE: Harris and Taylor (2008a).

TABLE 5-3 Additional Fixed Annual Costs of Standards, Assessment, and Accountability

	Cost of Annual Test Reviews
Florida	N/A
North Dakota	$61,000
Texas	$842,000

NOTE: N/A = Not available.
SOURCE: Harris and Taylor (2008a).

for preK-12 education are $15.5 billion for Florida, which has 2,539,929 students; $711.0 million for North Dakota, which has 104,225 students; and $28.2 billion for Texas, which has 4,259,823 students (http://www.edweek.org/rc/states/ [April 2008]).

Harris and Taylor cautioned that their figures are estimates, because of the many factors that complicated the analysis. For example, in some cases data were available in one state but not another, so they developed estimated figures. Nevertheless, despite significant differences among the three states, the per-student estimates were remarkably similar and provided a reasonable basis for national estimates. Adjusting for comparatively low cost-of-living averages in the three states studied, Harris and Taylor came up with an estimate of $124 to $173 as a range of per-student cost across the nation. Multiplying that by the nation's student population, they came up with a range of $6.1 to $8.5 billion as the total national expenditure on standards, assessment, and accountability.

TABLE 5-4 Total Fixed and Variable Costs for Three States ($ millions)

	Florida	North Dakota	Texas
Total fixed costs	$27	$1.4	$14.3
Total variable costs	$328.0	$12.9	$528.0
Fixed costs as a percentage of annual per pupil costs	7.6%	9.8%	2.6%

SOURCE: Harris and Taylor (2008a).

The next step was to estimate the cost impact of switching to a common system. For this analysis, Harris and Taylor broke down for the three states the fixed costs (e.g., the standards themselves, annual test reviews, and state assessment divisions), which stay the same regardless of the number of students served by the program, and the variable costs (e.g., testing contracts, professional development, local data management), which vary with the numbers of students involved. Estimates for these two types of costs are shown in Table 5-4.

From these numbers, Harris and Taylor were able to estimate the total cost savings of converting to a system of common standards: the range was 2.6 to 8 percent, or $183 to $850 million per year. Characterizing the saving as "pretty modest," Harris suggested that "we can conclude that the cost-savings issue is not going to be the main reason for going to a common system." However, he and Taylor also developed cost estimates for some of the activities that states undertake as part of standards-based accountability that are not required, such as conducting quarterly benchmarking assessments, developing higher quality (not machine scored) assessments, initiatives designed to support low-performing schools, and teacher performance incentives. These costs significantly increase the total cost of states' programs and may exceed the cost complying with current policies.

Harris pointed out that their estimates are significantly higher than others that have been suggested—about six times higher. He attributed this in part to the fact that theirs is the first to be developed following enactment of NCLB and thus includes the expanded requirements of that law. He and Taylor also included a broader range of state and local costs.

Harris and Taylor's portrait of the complexity of estimating costs and identifying potential savings that could be achieved with a model based on common standards stimulated a range of reactions. Discussant Thomas Toch was struck by how small the investment has been. He argued that standardized tests have become, by default, the central driver of standards-based reform, the mechanism that largely determines what is taught and when and how it is taught. Yet of the average $8,000 spent per pupil annually, only one-half of 1 percent goes toward building the tests that are to measure progress toward the high standards that are widely supported. From his perspective, a move to common standards and tests would, by reducing the significant financial burden to states of developing their own standards and assessment programs, free resources for other targeted investments in improving teaching and learning.

Discussant Susan Traiman also voiced concerns about the quality of the existing system. She questioned the usefulness of estimating the cost of producing systems that have received relatively low marks for quality, referring not just to the three states that were analyzed, but to all 50. She was also concerned that the approach Harris and Taylor used did not account for relative quality among states' standards, pointing out that a state with a smaller number of very focused, thoughtfully developed standards might have a higher per-standard cost than a state with a multitude of standards. She argued that a more critical question was what kinds of resources the nation and the states are willing to invest to make sure that all students meet rigorous standards.

Other participants added to this point, noting that of most interest would be a sense of the cost of developing common standards that had the effect of helping more students meet high standards. To calculate the cost in that way would mean including the costs for such interventions as professional development courses and new instructional materials.

Discussant Dave Driscoll pointed out additional costs that could be considered in light of the earlier discussion about resources and capacity. One example is the cost to Massachusetts of releasing every single test item that is used so that the process is completely transparent to students, parents, and the public: doing so increases the cost substantially (other states bank many items for reuse), but it has important political and practical benefits. Driscoll also noted that "at the beginning we had plenty of money . . . the legislature provided whatever we needed." Over time, however, budgets have been squeezed. The Massachusetts legislature had initially provided extra funds to support students who were in danger of failing the high school graduation test, but as first-time pass rates passed 80 percent, those funds were discontinued.

Discussant Mark Harris considered the capacity issue from a qualitative perspective. He observed that although states prize their autonomy and flexibility in developing systems that will best serve their students, many nevertheless base much of their instruction on commercially available programs that have very little connection to state standards. These programs are often designed to provide so-called teacher-proof curricula and instructional plans and thus do very little to develop the capacities of teachers who use them or to push the state-specific education goals forward.

Participants proposed many potential costs that had not been considered in the analysis, while acknowledging both the complexity involved in developing the estimates and their value as a starting point for discussion. Laurie Wise summed up the message that many drew from the consideration of costs with a reminder of the fundamental question: "Is what we are investing in actually helping students to meet these standards, not just in defining and measuring them?"

ESTIMATING THE COST OF EDUCATIONAL ADEQUACY

The estimates provided by Harris and Taylor were for the costs of developing and maintaining a standards-based system, but the ultimate purpose of these tasks is to provide every student with a so-called adequate education. Educational adequacy is a concept that has gained currency in the context of lawsuits that have been brought in many states to force their governments to address persistent inequalities in facilities and instruction. The question of what implications a move to common standards might have on adequacy lawsuits is addressed below. Lori Taylor explored the question of how one might measure educational adequacy and its costs.[2]

Although there is no firm consensus about how one should measure adequacy in an education context, there are two approaches that researchers use, she explained. One is a bottom-up analysis, in which the researchers try to define a model, or prototypical, school and then calculate what it would cost to replicate that school in all of the settings found in a particular state. This can be done either by asking experts to describe a school that will meet a set of performance standards (professional judgment method) or by considering what resources would be necessary to replicate the schools designed by whole-school reform models that have been proven effective by some agreed-upon metric (evidence-based method). These approaches have been used in just over half the states over the past decade.

Alternatively, top-down analyses examine the existing relationship between student performance, school expenditures, and other cost factors in a state and use those findings to predict the cost of meeting specified performance standards. One method is to use a variety of data on student performance to identify a set of schools that are successful and then

[2]Taylor's remarks were based on Baker, Taylor, and Vedlitz (2008).

predict that the cost of providing an adequate education is the average cost of providing education in those successful schools (successful school method). Another is to use cost and performance data from schools to estimate the relationship between expenditures and the prices of resources, student outcomes, and student need characteristics (such as the fraction of the study body that is receiving compensatory education for low socioeconomic status, school-district size, and any other variables that may affect the cost of providing education). The estimate of adequacy is the predicted cost of achieving designated outcomes in settings with particular local characteristics (cost function method). Fewer than 20 states have used one of these methods, and some have used both top-down and bottom-up approaches.

These various approaches yield somewhat different results, with the minimum cost of adequacy, in 1999 dollars, ranging from $3,000 to $9,000 per pupil. The highest estimates tend to come from the professional judgment studies, the lowest estimates tend to come from cost function studies, and results can differ even within states. For example, in Missouri, three types of studies have been done, with different results: the professional judgment method yielded an estimate of approximately $7,500, and the successful school and cost function methods both came in near $5,000 per pupil.

Taylor suggested several reasons for these differing results. First, there are differences in what the cost estimates actually represent. For example, researchers might have reported only an average of the total cost per district or per pupil, or they might have reported the base cost of regular education programs and treated separately the additional costs for special, bilingual, and compensatory education. The successful school method may be based on the average costs at schools that have relatively advantaged student populations, thus understating the actual costs of replication.

Another factor is differences in definitions of adequacy. As discussed earlier, states have widely divergent standards of proficiency, and definitions of adequacy may be pegged to those descriptions. Moreover, top-down estimates are based on a quantifiable standard that is already being achieved, while professional judgment studies develop estimates of performance standards that are not necessarily being achieved and are difficult to quantify.

Differences in school district size and student needs can also yield substantial differences in per-pupil costs, so differences in the ways these studies adjust for scale and need are another important source of variance. For example, Taylor pointed out, in Texas there are districts with fewer than 40 students. Thus the superintendent's salary and other fixed costs are divided by a very small number, which would contribute to a very high per-pupil estimate. Districts with high proportions of disadvantaged students, who require various supplementary services and resources, will also have higher costs, but these costs are typically not factored into successful school and evidence-based studies, whereas they are in cost function and professional judgment studies.

Even when adjustments are made, there are several methods of estimating the necessary adjustment, particularly with respect to the costs of educating disadvantaged students, which further contributes to the variation. A further complication is the intersection of the extra costs of educating underserved students with the proficiency level that is used as a bar. The differential cost of getting low-income students to a relatively low cut-point standard might be modest, but the differential cost of getting low-income students up to the proficiency standard might increase in a disproportionate way with higher and higher performance standards. Moreover, Taylor added, "we are using the same household income thresholds or poverty thresholds in New York City as we use in Dalhart, Texas." Thus, the instrument's ability to discriminate between truly needy children and moderately needy children is much stronger in some states than in others, which will lead to much stronger estimates of the differential costs of serving those students in some states than in others.

Finally, policy differences among states and districts affect the estimates as well. Policies regarding class size, length of the school day and year, teacher compensation, and other factors may mean large differences in the cost of providing services from one district to the next, which will in turn yield differences in the cost of adequacy.

There are strengths and weaknesses to each of these approaches to measuring adequacy, and, in Taylor's view, no single one of them is clearly superior either theoretically or practically. What is clear, she argued, is that increasing student performance will require either more resources, a reallocation of resources from some other purpose, or an increase in school efficiency. As a result, estimating the cost of meeting common standards would be a massive undertaking. Existing studies are not well designed to support an estimate of the cost of meeting common national standards. Ideally, this analysis would be done on a state-by-state basis, so that it could examine the ways existing state performance levels differ from the intended common performance standards, and factor in local prices, local union regulations, and the numerous other factors that affect the cost of education. Regardless of whether the analysis is done state by state, the choice of methodology is likely to affect the results, so multiple estimates would be more reliable than a single one. However, Taylor concluded, "all the estimates are likely to indicate a substantial increase in costs . . . potentially orders of magnitude greater than the actual costs of standards, assessments, and accountability."

Participants responded by discussing the way the question is framed politically—with most recognizing that saving money is not likely to be a persuasive reason for adopting common standards. One noted that the costs are really the costs of providing a good education, and that parceling out the elements as if some are optional may disguise the obligation. Another noted the complexity of making a political case for the benefits of increased spending for a policy approach. There are too many cases, such as the push to reduce class size, for which it was never possible to muster sufficient evidence to prove that the expenditure was worthwhile—and achievement gaps remained. The challenge is to sell the whole package—to make the case for a holistic approach to thinking about what constitutes a good education and side-stepping prolonged arguments about the costs and benefits of isolated strategies that are unlikely to be sufficient in themselves to have meaningful impact.

The two presentations dealt separately with the costs of complying with specific legal requirements and the costs of actually meeting standards. The fact that the analyses are so different highlights the equity implications of the relationship between funding, notions of what should be considered "good enough" for students, and how much both vary from state to state.

6

Political and Legal Considerations

The discussion of costs led naturally to a consideration of the political factors that would need to be considered if the nation were to move toward common standards and of the implications such a move might have for legal action regarding educational adequacy. Lorraine McDonnell provided a framework for thinking about political feasibility, and Goodwin Liu provided an overview of the implications for litigation.

POLITICAL FEASIBILITY

Any major policy change will impose political costs, McDonnell explained, and she suggested six factors that policy makers are likely to consider in deciding whether the educational and political benefits of moving to common standards outweigh the political as well as the financial costs. Her analysis was based on the recent history of similar education reforms, the theoretical and empirical literature on policy design, and interviews with leaders in the five states that were included in the analysis conducted by Massell, described in Chapter 2.

The first point to consider is what sort of common standards option is being suggested. Options that are more limited in scope and grow out of voluntary collaborations among, say, a small number of states are likely to impose fewer political costs than options that either are more comprehensive in scope or are perceived as having been imposed from above. Thus, the first of the six factors is the *perceptual element*, or how the change is framed. For example, is it presented as a solution to a specific problem that those involved believe needs to be solved? Is the common standard viewed as more or less rigorous than the standard it replaces? Will it be seen as imposing additional burdens, as No Child Left Behind (NCLB) did, or as a way to address the shortcomings of NCLB? Advocates of common standards, she argued, would be wise to consider the incentives for state policy makers to incur the political risks of making such a significant change.

State requirements for standards approval are another important factor. In most states, standards development and review require a multistep process. Ultimate authority generally rests with the state board of education, although in some cases the legislature must also sign off. However, many other participants influence the process in different ways. As the discussion about the quality of content standards illustrates, there is a tension between a broadly inclusive process and a more controlled one. The more broadly inclusive approach tends to engender less opposition than an approach that relies more heavily on expert opinion, and it is more consistent with democratic political values. The tradeoff, however, is that the standards developed through the more inclusive process may be less consistent and focused than those developed through a process shaped primarily by subject matter experts.

Moreover, the multistep process allows numerous opportunities for opponents of the idea to mobilize, which means that advocates would need to consider the *likelihood that groups will mobilize in support or opposition* to the change. Given the history of bitter disputes at the national and state levels over curricula, McDonnell found, many policy makers are unwilling to consider any change more drastic than modest, grassroots-based approaches to common standards.

Related, then, is the need for *policy entrepreneurs*, individuals, or groups who are willing to invest the time and political resources to make an active push for a policy goal. Many groups serve this function at the national level, although these groups may need to build state-level networks in order to get the issue on the agenda and shape perceptions of the proposed change. Such networks would also provide ways to anticipate the responses of groups likely to have strong reactions to a significant policy change. Without them, the political costs of the policy change are likely to be much greater.

McDonnell also pointed out that time and resource constraints often mean that policy makers pay limited attention to implementation issues when considering new policies. Yet, she explained, "we know from lots of research over 30 years that few policies reach schools and classrooms without significant modification. You can't mandate what matters in the classroom." Thus, policy makers need to consider *what will be required to implement the policy*, both practical and political efforts. Considerations include a state's existing capacity, the design of the initiative, and other state policy priorities that may compete for attention, as well training, support, expertise, and time for teachers to become truly comfortable with the changes they are being asked to make.

Along with the specific implementation requirements, advocates will need to consider one additional factor: the mismatch between political cycles and the *time frames* required for policies to be implemented and to produce their intended effects. This tension is evident with any kind of education policy, because it takes time to implement a policy fully, and then even more time for its effects to manifest themselves. But electoral cycles are two or four years, and elected officials often feel intense pressure to show results or take quick action to solve problems—even those that require longer term solutions. "The policy entrepreneurs who are thinking about common standards right now see an opening policy window. There is a question about how long that window is going to be open," McDonnell observed. At the same time, however, quick action to take advantage of that window may conflict with the goal of taking an incremental approach through which local capacity can be built gradually, and policy makers can be encouraged to embrace the approach in their own time. And of course, calculations related to timing may look different in different states.

McDonnell closed with the observation that, although none of these factors is an immutable obstacle to common standards, "federalism is a very powerful idea in this country. I just can't believe that any kind of common standards option or common standards movement is really going to alter this defining characteristic of U.S. education policy." Thus, whatever form common standards might take, her view is that they would be likely to have a unique profile in each state.

IMPLICATIONS FOR EDUCATIONAL ADEQUACY LITIGATION

Litigation over equity and adequacy has had a very significant effect on education policy over the past decade or so, and it is likely to have important implications for any move to common standards. Goodwin Liu provided an overview of the history of school finance litigation, the ways the issue of educational adequacy has been treated by the courts, and the relationship between legislated standards and adequacy lawsuits.

The first efforts to address educational inequities in the courts were federal suits brought during the 1960s and early 1970s, Liu explained. These were claims based on the equal protection clause of the 14th amendment to the U.S. Constitution, on the theory that financing education with property taxes created large disparities among population subgroups. A second wave of similar lawsuits was brought in state courts in the 1970s and 1980s. These cases were efforts to take advantage of a doctrine that was successful in the Supreme Court under Chief Justice Earl Warren: that there are positive social and economic rights implicit in the U.S. Constitution, such as the right to medical care, basic income, among others, as well as education.

In a 1973 ruling, however, *San Antonio Independent School District v. Rodriguez*, the Supreme Court found that the federal courts should not adjudicate issues of school finance equity. The Court reasoned that these cases are very complicated and involve too many unresolved questions, such as how equality should be defined. Would it mean equality of dollars? Of opportunity? Of material resources? Would it be measured by district, by school, or by students? Was the primary concern taxpayer equity or children's equity? In 1973, Liu pointed out, much of the research now available regarding the impact of spending on the quality of education had not yet been conducted. Moreover, he suggested, the principle of local control of public education had not yet been modified to make room for national or federal initiatives, such as standards-based reform or NCLB, so the idea of a federally determined standard of school finance equity would have seemed quite radical at that time. The *Rodriguez* decision did not, however, rule on the question of whether there is a federal constitutional right to an adequate education—and the court still has not done so.

In response to the *Rodriguez* ruling, plaintiffs turned to the state courts, with mixed results. The California Supreme Court found that the state's school finance system did violate the equal protection clause, and courts in Connecticut, Tennessee, and West Virginia were also receptive to that claim. Similar cases were rejected in other states, however, including Colorado, Illinois, Washington, and Wisconsin. In general, Liu explained, in states that had successful lawsuits, the result was that the districts that had been less well funded received modest boosts.

A third wave of lawsuits also targeted state courts, using a revised theoretical argument that focused on adequacy rather than equity. Liu suggested several factors that were responsible for this shift. First, adequacy theories were less radical in their implications than the equality-based argument, because equality is so difficult to define. Courts may have shied away from acknowledging equity as a right in part because it could potentially be unlimited, and it could be a precedent applicable in other contexts. Educational adequacy, however, could be defined by a threshold below which no one should be allowed to fall, and it was thus both less radical and less costly in its implications. It also seemed less likely to pit districts against one another.

The state courts have looked favorably on the adequacy arguments, pioneered in Kentucky in 1989 and in New Jersey in 1990: in 20 of 29 states in which such lawsuits have been filed since 1989, the plaintiffs have won. In these states, the courts have tended to define an adequate education in fairly broad terms, Liu noted—more expansively than NCLB has done. In Kentucky, for example, an adequate education was defined as one that provides every student with seven components, which include oral and written communication skills; knowledge of economic, social, and political systems; grounding in the arts; and others, but it does not include performance to a particular level on standardized assessments.

The result in Kentucky was the Kentucky Education Reform Act of 1990, which was an early model for the standards-based reform movement, but Liu noted that political momentum to embrace standards and reform the system had already existed in that state prior to the ruling. In New Jersey and Ohio, in contrast, the legislatures did not act as quickly or decisively, and the courts have acknowledged the limits to their power to bring about change. The courts have, however, generally attempted to monitor the states' responses to the rulings, and the Massachusetts Supreme Court recently relinquished its jurisdiction on the grounds that the state had fully complied with the legal requirement.

Liu offered some comments about the relationship between the courts' definitions of adequacy and other kinds of standards that states adopt through some sort of democratic process. One might expect that state-developed standards would provide a ready resource for courts because they represent what the people of the state have defined as acceptable guidelines. However, state standards tend to be far more narrowly focused than judicial definitions of educational adequacy. "Judges don't want to tie themselves to the mast of just reading, math, and science. They have a broader vision of education in mind," Liu explained. Moreover, test scores that can meet legislated standards sometimes obscure other kinds of inequalities—there may be significant inequality among the group of students who can pass a minimum cut point, for example. There may also be inequality in the curriculum and instruction that is brought about by testing requirements. Students in a low-performing school may be focused on "drill and kill" to get them over a certain score level, while other students receive a much richer education. And making particular performance standards the legal requirement may give legislatures a perverse incentive to lower the standards and impoverish education for all students.

Thus, Liu concluded, standards are likely to continue to be informative to the courts but not to be adopted by them as legal standards, regardless of whether they are developed at the state or the national level. Moreover, standards are not likely to influence the courts except as they are filtered through an individual state's education system. He also believes that standards that are articulated as means of providing for equality of opportunity and of maintaining the political and social fabric are more likely to be compelling to the courts than are standards defined as means of maintaining economic competitiveness for a state or for the nation. "Courts," he explained, "do not believe it is their role to think about whether or not the nation or the state is adequately competitive relative to the rest of the country." They do regard it as their role to safeguard the democratic system of government, which relies on responsible voters, jurors, and citizens, and on social stability, which in turn depends on the existence of sufficient guarantees of fairness in individual opportunity.

Liu's closing thought was that, although the current U.S. Supreme Court seems unlikely to enter into the question of whether the U.S. Constitution guarantees some fundamental right to educational adequacy, that may change in time. Any effort to litigate this claim could succeed, in Liu's view, only if sufficient groundwork had been laid in developing public consensus as to what constitutes educational adequacy. The cooperation necessary to develop common standards could serve as a critical element in developing a consensus that would reassure the Court that it was not going far out on limb in finding a right to educational adequacy.

7

Perspectives on Common Standards

Questions about the effects a move to common standards might have and about which issues would deserve the highest priority if this policy initiative were undertaken may look different to people with different perspectives on education policy and practice. The committee thus invited discussants representing three important perspectives—researchers, elected officials, and implementers—to reflect on the advantages and disadvantages of the options for common standards, asking them to use the options and evaluation framework described in Chapter 3 to structure the conversation. This discussion was preceded by a look at two examples of what discussant Lynn Olson described as an existence proof that shared standards can be successful.

TWO EXAMPLES

The idea of common standards across ages and subjects for the nation is thus far largely hypothetical, but two programs provide examples of efforts to share standards. The end-of-course exam in algebra II being developed by Achieve as part of the American Diploma Project, and the New England Common Assessment Program (NECAP) are both cases in which groups of states are implementing shared standards in the context of assessment programs. Matthew Gandal described the Achieve project and Peter McWalters described NECAP.

Achieve

Achieve did not set out to develop common standards, Gandal explained, although the organization was founded as a way for states to compare notes and benchmark their efforts as they pursued standards-based reform. As part of that work, Achieve has provided evaluations of states' standards and assessments, comparing them in terms of their rigor and other characteristics. Achieve collaborated with the Fordham Foundation, the Education Trust, and the National Alliance of Business to launch the American Diploma Project (ADP), which initially focused on defining the core skills young people need to succeed in college and the workplace. Ultimately, the group developed specific benchmarks in English and mathematics as a more concrete guide to the states that joined the ADP network. That network, which now includes 32 states, asks each member state to sign on to a program of aligning standards, assessments, graduation requirements, and data and accountability systems at the K-12 level with postsecondary and workplace expectations, as exemplified in the ADP benchmarks.

Achieve has worked with 20 of the participating states to update their standards and align them with the ADP benchmarks and with the expectations of the postsecondary institutions and employers in the states. They have found that a common core of knowledge and skills is increasingly shared across these states. Individual states may vary in the ways they present their standards, in the weight they attach to different elements, and in other ways, but the core has become increasingly easy to see, Gandal explained.

Recognizing the critical role played by assessments, Achieve has also worked with 13 states to oversee the development of an algebra II assessment designed to be used at the end of the course. The participating states recognized that they were emphasizing the same material and that it would be logical to work together to develop a high-quality test. Interestingly, Gandal noted, ironing out the procurement procedures across the states so that they could join forces in hiring a testing contractor was in some ways more challenging than hammering out the content and performance expectations.

For Gandal, the experience has been a heartening proof of what is possible: "If states, working collaboratively, can agree on common standards and develop assessments in common, they could actually accomplish some of what you have been talking about in this room, which is ultimately coming up with a common expectation and measuring it."

New England Common Assessment Program

The process Achieve has gone through with algebra II bears some striking similarities to NECAP, which is a collaboration among New Hampshire, Rhode Island, and Vermont. The departments of education in these states have developed grade-level expectations and test specifications in reading, writing, mathematics, and science. In New Hampshire, NECAP is administered in grades 3-8 and 11 in mathematics and reading, and in grades 5, 8, and 11 in writing. Science was administered for the first time in May 2008, in grades 4, 8, and 11. Results are reported on a common scale.

McWalters, the commissioner of education for Rhode Island, explained that his state was eager to collaborate with its neighbors because it is very small and demographically disadvantaged in comparison to its neighbors. Moreover, he joked, "in anything we do, we always come out the lowest in New England." Education leaders in Rhode Island were not satisfied with the state's existing standards. The collaboration was relatively easy to establish, he added, because in all three of the states the department of education had the authority to modify or replace the academic standards.

In McWalters's view, one of the most important benefits of the program has been the political cover it has provided for the tensions that arise when any state attempts to raise expectations for students. The NECAP assessments were more challenging in many respects than the ones Rhode Island had used previously, and as a result some of the early results, particularly those for secondary mathematics, were disappointingly low. However, as these results came out, he explained, "nobody blinked." The leaders from the three states were resolute in resisting pressure to lower the proficiency cut points. McWalters observed that the states' decision was vindicated, since their NECAP results now line up well with those from the National Assessment of Educational Progress assessments.

Based on the success of NECAP thus far, McWalters is optimistic about the potential benefits of incremental collaboration of this sort, arguing that states should "keep sharing, keep finding those opportunities when systems are about to go through their review anyway. But use systems like Achieve to find others that are close enough—don't drag in the lowest one on the national ranking and the highest one." Moreover, he believes that the process has highlighted the biggest unaddressed problem in New Hampshire and around the country, which is the reality that different sets of students are held to different expectations and provided with different sets of opportunities. "Once you get past the sixth grade, and even on our NECAP test, you can see the cohort starting to flatten, because we are starting to track [students] in middle school. Once you start tracking in this high-standards environment, you have students who have never seen the content on the test." An accountability system that is not also a capacity-building system cannot solve that problem.

RESEARCHERS

Three researchers, Andrew Isaacs, Brain Rowan, and William Schmidt, offered their perspectives. Andrew Isaacs focused on challenges to some of the assumptions he thought had undergirded much of the discussion. He described as "wobbly" the proposition that "a more centralized national curriculum would lead to higher student achievement, and that higher student achievement in turn would lead to increased economic competitiveness." He pointed out that the United States is one of only a handful of countries that does not have a national curriculum—and that not only countries that outperform it by whatever measure, but also most countries that perform less well, have a national curriculum. Moreover, a variety of other factors—such as teacher quality, family influences, and respect for education—seem likely to have just as powerful an effect as the curriculum. Isaacs also argued that the policies of the Federal Reserve Bank and other factors are likely to have far more significant effects on the nation's economic performance than the nature of its standards and curricula.

He also challenged the idea that the variability in grade level expectations is a significant problem, because he believes it generally reflects the lack of a research basis, in many cases, for placing a particular topic at a particular grade level. Despite that, there is "an awful lot of uniformity already in the math curriculum." His fear was that if the curriculum is very tightly controlled, innovation will be discouraged. Moreover, he suggested, the so-called math wars are continuing, so if there is just one curriculum, there is the chance that it could go in an unproductive direction, as he suggested it has in California.

With regard to the framework, his view was that if the nation were to pursue common standards, a trusted national group, such as the National Governors Association, not the federal government, should lead the effort, and it should be allowed to develop slowly, to provide time for natural collaboration. In his opinion, "other subjects need this a lot more than mathematics—in mathematics we have a huge amount of agreement about what should be taught."

Brain Rowan organized his observations of public education around inputs, outputs, and process, arguing that the nation has been focusing on the first two at the expense of the last. Since the nation's education bureaucracy was founded, he argued, people have been working on input standards: "we have adequacy studies and rules about teacher certification, and about how kids get to school, and so forth." More recently, the nation has developed "a fairly elaborate, if imperfect, system of output controls," particularly through the assessment requirements associated with the Elementary and Secondary Education Act and the No Child Left Behind Act.

However, he argued, "we don't have any professional or even bureaucratically consensual rules about how to turn these inputs into outputs." In Rowan's view, what is missing is an adequate investment in evidence-based practice, as used in the practice of medicine. If a policy shift is to be pursued, he would advocate reducing spending on assessment and accountability systems and using the savings to build knowledge of how to improve outputs—outcomes for students. This could be done, for example, by relying more on adaptive testing and sampling—collecting fewer data overall and focusing on the information that could be useful in specific ways to the enterprise of improving student learning.

In Rowan's view, "scientifically, the worst-case scenario would be for the United States to settle on a single national test." He believes that having a variety of tests makes it possible to evaluate evidence on particular hypotheses. He believes that "a diversity of standards, of processes, and of tests would generate more hypotheses and better evidence than would a system that only had one way of doing business."

William Schmidt used the elements of the evaluation framework—quality, equity, feasibility, and opportunity costs—to reinforce several points. First, he stressed the critical importance of the sequence in which topics are covered, saying, "it is not arbitrary. You can't just flow through topics around and across grades." He argued that there are very big differences in the degree to which state standards are coherent in the way that mathematicians would define coherence. Furthermore, "no other country in the world that I am familiar with has this conversation about alignment, because they don't even think there would be any alternative to [an aligned system]."

The result is a lack of equity. He argued that it is unreasonable to expect to eliminate black-white gaps and gaps between students with low and high socioeconomic status, until the causes of the inequity in students' educational opportunities are addressed. He finds it appalling that the United States tolerates the reality that different groups of children are offered very different content, at least in mathematics and science.

Thus, rather than worrying about the cost of moving toward common standards, he suggested considering instead the cost of not doing so. "There are huge costs there. We face them every day. We hear about them from the business world."

ELECTED OFFICIALS

Julie Bell, Rae Ann Kelsch, and Roy Romer commented, each from a different vantage point, on the way elected officials may look at the question of common standards. Julie Bell began by explaining that her organization, the National Conference of State Legislatures (NCSL) represents not just individual representatives but the 50 legislatures, and that they are entirely bipartisan. Thus their mission is not to advocate policy positions to the states, but to support the legislative process by providing information and analysis. Nevertheless, the NCSL has opposed NCLB because its members took the position that the law's provisions were not an appropriate role for the federal government in education policy.

Thus, with respect to the question of common standards the NCSL's members are very interested in the possibilities for improvements, but they have a great deal of concern about how such a policy could be national but not federal, worrying that the federal government would be "tempted . . . to jump in and take control."

Deep concern about global economic competitiveness is dominating discussion of education in legislatures around the country, Bell explained. State officials are worried about the variability in educational opportunity, but they tend to focus on evening things out in their own states, rather than at the national level. She also has found that standards are not a primary focus for legislators, who are more interested in issues they see as more "tangible . . . teaching quality and spending and top quality school leaders who can make a difference for schools."

For Rae Ann Kelsch, a state representative from North Dakota, the first observation was that legislators are very interested in what they hope to gain from a given investment. She noted that the workshop discussion "zipped right into 'how do we implement the standards, how do we go about developing the standards?' before identifying what are we trying to achieve if we go to a common standards approach in the United States." Will this approach improve graduation rates, raise achievement levels, or get more kids into college, for example?

She thought legislators would be very interested in some of the potential benefits she heard described at the workshop. The idea of having consistent information, so that the significance of comparative data about students is clear, is very appealing. She thought her colleagues would be very interested, for example, in the data showing that North Dakota students perform less well on NAEP than on the state's own assessments. And legislators are likely to be in favor of opportunities to avoid costly mistakes—not to have to "go through what other states went through the first time they developed new standards."

Kelsch also observed that the concept of standards is not particularly well understood in her state—and that the idea that the state needs to prepare to compete economically with other nations is only beginning to take root. Consequently, residents and legislators tend to think their standards are fine as they are and to be relatively uninterested in what other states may be doing. So the preliminary reaction to the idea of common standards may be "it would be okay if we adopted common standards, as long as they were my common standards."

Roy Romer, former governor of Colorado, acknowledged the challenges of building understanding of the challenges the nation faces in improving education for all students, saying that "we have got to bring to America an awareness of the peril that they are in." He believes that Americans are genuinely worried that "their eighth grader is not going to be able to afford the house they now live in, or send their children to college." While many may see that the answer to that worry is to build skills and knowledge, consensus about the urgency and the strategy to address it has not yet been forged.

What is the best mechanism for making common standards a reality? Romer suggested starting with two or three models as experiments, taking some time to develop evidence about what is successful, and allowing others to observe the benefits. He acknowledged the profound skepticism regarding the federal government's involvement but believes that the U.S. Department of Education can provide invaluable support, supplying states with the tools they need to move forward on their own. Rather than responding to federal mandates, he argued, states should be benchmarking their performance annually against that of the 10 best nations in the world. Here again, the federal government can facilitate that effort and supply resources without serving as an enforcer.

Romer agreed with earlier observations that testing is driving the current system in unhelpful ways, but argued that testing still plays a critical role. States need better information from testing and higher quality assessments that have a more positive impact. But states cannot do this alone; "it is just too expensive." The primary value of a common standards approach for Romer is that the necessary improvements cannot be accomplished at the school or even the district level. State legislatures need to undergo a paradigm shift, to see that collaboration offers them a valuable opportunity, rather than the burden of being told what to do.

IMPLEMENTERS

The three panelists who were asked to reflect on implementation issues were David Driscoll, James Liebman, and Richard Patz. As commissioner of education in Massachusetts, Driscoll oversaw the development of the state's curriculum frameworks, implementation of the Massachusetts Comprehensive Assessment System (MCAS), and state accountability assessment and development administration of new teacher licensure regulations. He described what he saw as the most important implementation issues, beginning with political consensus. In Massachusetts, he explained, "the stars lined up. The business community led it, the governor was behind it, the legislature was behind it—Republicans, Democrats. The people in Massachusetts were ready. They saw that we had a problem."

With the goal established, the next step was to develop the specific "carrots and sticks" that brought about specific changes. The state was willing to fund the improvements it wanted, allocating $2 billion in new monies between 1993 and 2000. Massachusetts also attached new accountability measures to the initiatives, starting with a tenth grade test that students would have to pass in order to graduate. Setting the pass score for this test was a delicate task, Driscoll noted: "it is like being a safecracker; you have got to get it just right." There was a push to set a high, meaningful standard, but the fear was that if too many students failed, the initiative would sink.

Driscoll agreed with Romer that "we are sleeping through a crisis." He believes the evidence is very clear that other countries hold their students to higher standards and that the United States will struggle to compete financially so long as that is true. Yet the nation has not had the will to change the schools. "If Horace Mann came down on earth today, the only institutions he would recognize are our schools." Because no one has rethought the school schedule, for example, during the past century, "we dump millions of kids into the streets of Detroit and Miami at 2:30 in the afternoon with nothing to do and no supervision." We offer them virtually nothing during the summer, and they come back in September having forgotten all that they learned." Yet solutions to these problems have already been figured out, and schools could be taking advantage of them.

Driscoll believes the U.S. president can begin the work of creating a sense of urgency about this issue, and that a commission, akin to the 9-11 Commission, could develop a specific plan. He believes states are "not all that far apart in their thinking about what kids should know and be able to do. The questions are about how high you set the standards." He also believes that the cost of setting common standards would not be prohibitive. The high cost will come with the changes required to get all students up to that standard. This will include two main elements: supports for struggling students (such as summer school, after school, and special education and psychological services) and real improvements in instruction. Driscoll illustrated the point with an observation about how amazed foreign educators are when they visit U.S. classrooms. School leaders from other countries may have sophisticated systems for guiding teachers and helping them improve, but principals in the United States tend to focus on external features, or, as Rowan suggested earlier, the inputs: "You are doing a nice job, nice bulletin boards, you vary your instruction nicely, you've got some nice little overheads there, you are using the smart board." Meanwhile, opportunities to figure out better ways to help the students who are falling behind are missed.

James Liebman brought to the discussion his perspective as chief accountability officer for the New York City Department of Education, and largely seconded Driscoll's comments. He described the approach in New York City, which has been to use standards and accountability to centralize the definitions of what students should learn, but to use a variety of strategies to empower schools to accomplish that goal. He believes that the central authority, whether the U.S. Department of Education, a state agency, or a district, should set initial, provisional learning goals and commit to revising the goals, once experience shows what is possible.

This balance of power, in which local entities (schools, districts, or states) have the authority to make some of their own decisions but are strictly accountable for the results, works best, he explained, when these entities see that they are being compared with their peers. Thus, in New York, the performance of the best school of a particular type becomes the standard that all other schools of that type need to meet. The other schools believe they can meet it because one of their own has done it.

The city grades schools, rewarding those that succeed and sanctioning those that fall behind in various ways. It offers comprehensive training in data management, performance management, and knowledge management, as well as a diagnostic assessment program that helps schools understand the data and use them to make improvements.

Liebman observed that "regression analyses don't work." The data on which schools (or districts or states) are evaluated has to be transparent so that it is easy for them to calculate and track their performance. In order to compare like entities to like entities without complex regression analyses, he suggested, one can use simple matching strategies using, say, five or six of the criteria that would go into the regression. Focusing on longitudinal student progress, rather than proficiency scores, is also important. "Low-performing students tend to progress further," Liebman explained. So measuring their progress "helps to balance out the proficiency bonus that the states with high-performing kids get."

Liebman's suggestion for pursuing common standards was that the federal government or some prestigious private entity could set provisional standards, perhaps only in a few subjects at first, and then establish a very clear grading system that focuses on both proficiency and growth to compare the performance of similar states. The focus would be on outcomes, not on the way states decide to establish their standards, but Liebman advocated rewarding states that perform well, progressively taking money or support away from those that do poorly and don't improve.

Finally, Richard Patz, vice president of research at CTP McGraw-Hill, offered the perspective of long-time education publisher. He has seen the textbook publishing and test development industry change significantly in response to NCLB. While the states are now all required to focus on reading and mathematics in grades 3 through 8, he explained, the differences from state to state in terms of both content standards and testing practices have increased.

The need to respond to this very varied market has meant that the publishers' work is very inefficient and far less profitable for testing companies than many people believe. In Patz's view, "building custom state tests to custom standards in a completely unique way in each state overall is just spending a lot of money that you would not have to spend if . . . there were some consensus around standards. It is very hard to leverage what we are doing in one state in another context."

Moreover, he believes that "you can do measurement in a much better way than it is currently being done, where we ask all 500,000 California fifth graders the same 40 or 45 questions." Computer adaptive testing is an excellent example. In most states there are too many students and too few computers to do it on a large scale, as the annual proficiency requirements of NCLB dictate. However, this technology could allow assessment of much broader domains, which could facilitate benchmark reference assessment, as well as matrix sampling of student populations, to facilitate more informative comparisons of their progress.

Patz is in a position to see the effects of the significant differences in the quality of states' standards and assessments. He believes that states underutilize the testing information they now have, and that with different, better information, they could answer more important questions—and better understand not just which teacher has higher performing students, but more about why, which programs and textbooks work best, and so forth. Nevertheless, he stressed that states that want to do these things well must be prepared to spend what it takes.

8

Concluding Reflections

The two workshops provided a wide array of factual information about current state standards and the way they have been implemented, as well as wide-ranging discussion of lessons that can be drawn from that information and the possibilities for taking the theory of standards in a new direction. Both workshops provided opportunities for participants to deliberate about what they had heard and for discussants to pull together the primary threads. North Carolina Governor James Hunt provided closing thoughts as well.

SYNTHESIS

As the conversation evolved over the two workshops, several key points emerged from the presentations and discussions.

First, there seemed to be wide acknowledgment that *standards are now an accepted part of the educational landscape and that they play multiple roles in public education*. Moreover, standards are seen as very important—and the need to improve them is seen as critical—because they are viewed as a means of achieving educational equity. However, the discussion suggested that neither the precise role that standards play nor their effects have been adequately documented.

A number of comments reinforced the idea that one reason for the lack of clear answers about the effects of standards is that *there is no consistent definition of standards and standards-based reform*. States' approaches to standards vary in many critical ways, not least in quality. Presenters and participants cited rigor, specificity, focus, and coherent learning progressions as critical aspects of high-quality standards, but there is no widely shared conception of quality or of the essential components of standards-based reform.

The current system is characterized by dramatic variation. There is significant variability among states in the nature of their content standards, what is covered, and the performance levels they set. It is not entirely clear what effects this variation has, although some view the variation itself as a major impediment to equity. Moreover, there may be as much variation in the ways different districts in a state implement standards (perhaps even among classrooms in a school) as there is among states.

It is also not clear whether common standards for states would reduce this variability. The variation in proficiency standards highlights the limitations of a model that focuses on achievement to a particular defined level. Many argue that a growth model (an assessment system that focuses on measuring students' academic growth over time) may be a more useful approach than a model that provides snapshots of the percentages of students who have reached a particular level.

The variability in the implementation of standards-based reforms among states may reflect the lack of consensus about what good standards look like. Some noted, for example, that there is no obvious relationship between the coverage of content and performance on common measures, such as the National Assessment of Educational Progress (NAEP). Others viewed the variation as a critical obstacle to the equality of opportunity that is a key goal of standards-based reform efforts. In some ways, assessments and proficiency scores have come to stand in for academic content standards, but few see this as a positive development. Many people believe that test-based accountability has made the goal of proficiency dwarf far more important education goals. Poor student outcomes should raise questions about the adequacy of curriculum, instruction, classroom materials, the structure of the school day and year, leadership, and other factors in education. Thus, for example, the goal of 100 percent proficiency by 2014 may be far less useful than establishing firm standards for states related to students' opportunity to learn.

The current system of standards is not working as it was intended to. The theory of standards-based reform was that if standards, assessments, and accountability systems were in place, everything else that needed to happen would follow. It seems clear now that this formulation was incomplete—that it omitted two critical factors. First, it did not directly address teaching itself and the mechanisms through which teachers would adapt their instruction. Second, it did not address the need for political will to address the disparities in the educational opportunities offered to students in different settings by making the needed broader changes. Comments demonstrated widespread agreement that the lack of will to push beyond the mechanics of standards documents and assessments and make fundamental changes in the way diverse students are served seems to be the reason that systemic reform has not been fully implemented in any state. Strategies for building on what has been accomplished through standards-based reform, such as a push for common standards, will need to take on those issues if they are to make a meaningful difference.

However, it is now widely recognized that insufficient attention was paid to how the desired changes would come about. In trying to effect change, states can offer guidance, pressure, and support, but many may be focusing on the pressure and not paying enough attention to the need for guidance and support.

Many also argue that *assessment has become the principal driver of most states' standards-based reform efforts.* The result of this unintended development has been a reduced focus on the broader goals for instruction and learning that are at the heart of standards-based reform as it was originally envisioned. Defining rigor is straightforward if the focus is on the numbers of students who meet a particular proficiency standard at a fixed date, but if states shift their focus to students' development and learning over time, they will need to develop more flexible learning expectations.

Thus, *consistent standards may be a necessary tool for ensuring educational equity, but simply establishing them will not accomplish the goal.* As long as performance standards and content standards are not integrated, the result is likely to be more of the same variability and inequity. Moreover, both teacher quality and focused textbook content are additional significant factors that would not be directly addressed by more uniform standards. Without them, no real improvement is likely.

There are significant practical obstacles to implementing common standards. For example, to what depth is uniformity necessary? By what process would common standards be developed, and who would be involved? Possibilities include collaborations among states, federal involvement, and third-party leadership, but even settling on the most desirable approach could be contentious. By all accounts, to have any chance of success, a common system would have to be voluntary. The effort may require some third party (other than state or federal policy makers) to sustain the effort across political cycles and to serve as an impartial broker of competing interests, but no obvious candidate for that role is apparent.

Common standards would not be a promising strategy for saving money, but the significant costs are those of providing a decent education, regardless of the overarching policy strategy. Although the estimated costs of standards-based reform and associated activities are higher than commonly recognized, they are still a minor fraction of education spending, especially relative to their importance. On one hand, a system of common standards might yield some savings, in economies of scale, but these savings would not amount to a persuasive argument for this approach. On the other hand, addressing the shortfalls in states' capacity to implement all of the elements of standards-based reform, irrespective of whether they are state or national systems, would require significant increased spending.

Advocates of common standards would do well to consider the political landscape carefully. Many seemed to agree that a bottom-up, grassroots approach to common standards would be the most likely to succeed, but such an effort may take time. Others argue that a political window is opening now, and that moving forward even with an incomplete and imperfect approach would be preferable to missing that window, given urgent pressure to address the glaring inequities in educational opportunity in the United States. Past efforts to set standards, including contentious efforts in individual disciplines (e.g., U.S. history), more recent efforts (such as Achieve's focus on algebra II for all), and the experience of states that have collaborated (e.g., the three New England states) offer valuable background for any plan to push for common K-12 standards.

The most basic political tension is that between the long-standing U.S. tradition of local control and the urge to tackle national problems with central solutions. NCLB has opened the door to a significantly heightened federal role, but states have been very resistant to many of its provisions. It is not clear at present whether a greater degree of commonality would be accepted by states. Nevertheless, it is likely that whatever form common standards might take, states will retain the prerogative to put their own stamp on them and implement then in their own ways.

The framing of the issue is likely to be key to its success. If states view common standards as a promising way to address problems that they perceive themselves as having, they are likely to sign on.

The establishment of common standards is not likely to lead to a new rush of adequacy or equity lawsuits. A close reading of court rulings shows that the goals they identify for education are much broader than the kinds of content and performance standards states now use or that would be suitable for common standards. The courts are interested in citizenship and the broad parameters of knowledge and understanding that young people need. They might be influenced by common standards to inform the debate, but the specifics are unlikely to shape court rulings.

CLOSING THOUGHTS

Hunt closed the workshop series with his thoughts on the critical importance of moving to common standards, describing this effort as "absolutely essential" to ensuring that the United States continues to prosper economically and to flourish as a nation.

He described the serious threat to the nation's economy of allowing significant numbers of students to grow up without an adequate education. Noting that in his home state of North Carolina, "We are graduating only 56 percent of our students who start in the ninth grade." He described the gloomy outcomes for those left behind, both as individuals and for society. A local company, the Bridgestone Tire Company, he said, must interview 100 local high school graduates to find one who meets their hiring requirements. Companies that have been outsourcing increasingly desirable technical jobs to other nations, he said, report that these competing workers are not only less expensive, but also every bit as well qualified or better than those available in the United States.

To ensure prosperity and equity for Americans, then, it is essential that the nation develop its workers so that they can compete—and for him that means establishing common standards so that all students will have access to a high-quality education and will be held to consistent standards.

He identified the four elements he believes will be crucial to making this goal a reality.

Leadership is critical. He cited his experience with the development of the National Board for Professional Teaching Standards in the 1980s to explain how important it is that those with competing views come together to work out differences and settle on a common approach—and as evidence that it can be done. It is critical to involve a range of players, including state legislators and teachers unions, but some entity will have to take the lead. A commission or an existing organization that is viewed as neutral, for example, could shepherd the process effectively.

The federal government must play a role. Certainly the federal government cannot and should not impose common standards on the states, but it does have a critical role to play, in his view. The next president could spotlight the importance of the issue. The federal government could provide meaningful subsidies to states to assist them in building the necessary capacity to implement the improvements that are so urgently needed.

Significant private financing will be needed. The federal government cannot be expected to finance the entire effort. Foundations play a very valuable role in stimulating and supporting education reforms, and a firm commitment will be needed in this case as well.

Public support must be mobilized. Hunt argued that the public has not been made sufficiently aware of the deficiencies of the education many of the nation's students are receiving. In his view, if people were aware of the deficiencies and of the risks they pose, they would support the sacrifices and disruption necessary to realign the system.

The governor was clear in his estimation of the importance of the challenge, saying "I think this is so serious that the only analogy I can think of is World War II."

References

American Federation of Teachers. (2003). *Setting Strong Standards.* Washington, DC: Author.

Baker, B., Taylor, L., and Vedlitz, A. (2008). *Adequacy estimates and the implications of common standards for the cost of instruction.* Report to the National Research Council, May 30, 2008.

Carr, P. (2008). *Comparing state proficiency standards using NAEP.* Presentation to the National Research Council Workshop on Assessing the Role of K-12 Academic Standards in States. Available: http://www7.nationalacademies.org/cfe/Carr%20Presentation.pdf [May 2008].

Center on Education Policy. (2007). *Answering the question that matters most: Has student achievement increased since No Child Left Behind?* Washington, DC: Center on Education Policy.

Editorial Projects in Education. (2008). *Quality Counts.* Bethesda, MD: Author.

Goertz, M.E. (2007). *Standards-based reform: Lessons from the past, directions for the future.* Paper presented at Clio at the Table: A Conference on the Uses of History to Inform and Improve Education Policy, Brown University.

Goertz, M.E. (2008). *Identifying the costs of standards-based K-12 education.* Presentation to the National Research Council Workshop on Assessing the Role of K-12 Academic Standards in States. Available: http://www7.nationalacademies.org/cfe/Goertz%20State%20Standards%20Presentation.pdf [April 2008].

Gross, P.R., Goodenough, U., Lerner, L.S., Haack, S., Schwartz, M., Schwartz, R., and Finn, Jr., C.E. (2005). *The state of state science standards.* Thomas B. Fordham Institute. Available: http://www.edexcellence.net/doc/Science%20Standards.FinalFinal.pdf [April 2008].

Harris, D., and Taylor, L. (2008a). Presentation to the National Research Council Workshop on Evaluating the Options for Common Standards. Available: http://www7.nationalacademies.org/cfe/Harris%20and%20Taylor%20Presentation.pdf [June 2008].

Harris, D., and Taylor, L. (2008b). *The resource costs of standards, assessments, and accountability*. Paper prepared for the National Research Council Workshop on Evaluating the Options for Common Standards. Available: http://www7.nationalacademies.org/cfe/HarrisTaylor%20Paper.pdf [June 2008].

Massell, D. (2008). *The current status and role of standards-based reform in the United States*. Paper prepared for the National Research Council Workshop on Assessing the Role of K-12 Academic Standards in States. Available: http://www7.nationalacademies.org/cfe/Massell%20State%20Standards%20Paper.pdf [May 2008].

National Center for Education Statistics. (2007). *Mapping 2005 state proficiency standards onto the NAEP scales*. Research and Development Report. Available: http://nces.ed.gov/nationsreportcard/pubs/studies/2007482.asp [April 2008].

National Commission on Excellence in Education. (1983). *A nation at risk*. Washington, DC: Author.

National Research Council. (2000). *How people learn: Brain, mind, experience, and school*. Committee on Developments in the Science of Learning, John D. Bransford, Ann L. Brown, and Rodney R. Cocking, eds. Washington, DC: National Academy Press.

National Research Council. (2001). *Adding it up: Helping children learn mathematics*. Mathematics Learning Study Committee, Jeremy Kilpatrick, Jane Swafford, and Bradford Findell, eds. Washington, DC: National Academy Press.

National Research Council. (2006). *Systems for state science assessment*. Committee on Test Design for K-12 Science Achievement, Mark R. Wilson and Meryl W. Bertenthal, eds. Washington, DC: The National Academies Press.

Petrilli, M. (2008). Presentation to the National Research Council Workshop on Assessing the Role of K-12 Academic Standards in States. Available: http://www7.nationalacademies.org/cfe/Petrilli%20Presentation.pdf [April 2008].

Porter, A., Polikoff, M., and Smithson, J. (2008). *Is there a de facto national curriculum? Evidence from state standards*. Paper prepared for the National Research Council Workshop on Assessing the Role of K-12 Academic Standards in States. Available: http://www7.nationalacademies.org/cfe/Porter_Smithson%20State%20Standards%20Paper_Tables.pdf [May 2008].

Smith, M.S., and O'Day, J. (1991). Systemic school reform, in S.H. Fuhrman and B. Malen, eds. *The politics of curriculum and testing*. Yearbook of the Politics of Education Association. New York: Falmer Press.

Appendix A

January 2008 Workshop Agenda and Participants

Workshop on Assessing the Role of K-12 Academic Standards in States
January 17-18, 2008

AGENDA

THURSDAY, JANUARY 17, 2008

8:00 am **Continental Breakfast**

8:30 am **Introduction and Goals of Workshop Series**
Michael Feuer, National Research Council Division of Behavioral and Social Sciences and Education
Judith Rizzo, James B. Hunt, Jr. Institute for Educational Leadership and Policy
Lorraine McDonnell, University of California at Santa Barbara, Workshop Series Steering Committee Chair

SESSION 1: SETTING THE STATE STANDARDS POLICY CONTEXT

Orienting the event's discussions in an analysis of existing literature and new research results on contemporary state standards-based reform efforts in California, Florida, Massachusetts, North Dakota, and Texas.

Framing Questions

1. What are the major roles that standards play in state K-12 education policy and practice?

2. What are the major strengths and weaknesses of K-12 state standards-based reform efforts with respect to achieving efficiency, equity, and quality? What are states doing to achieve these goals?
3. How and to what degree are the strengths and weaknesses of reform efforts related to the standards themselves? How and to what degree have the standards changed other education policies in states?
4. How and to what degree are the strengths and weaknesses of reform efforts related to having unique state standards?

9:00 am **Introduction and Goals of Session**
Lorraine McDonnell

9:15 am **Roles, Impacts, and Perceptions of Standards: Review of Existing Research and Results from Elite Policy Maker Interviews in California, Florida, Massachusetts, North Dakota, and Texas**
Diane Massell, University of Michigan

9:45 am **Moderated Discussion, Part 1: Research Perspectives**
Moderator: Lorraine McDonnell

Panelists:
Lynn Olson, *Education Week*
Brian Stecher, RAND Corporation

10:45 am **Break**

11:00 am **Moderated Discussion, Part 2: Policy and Practice Perspectives**
Moderator: Lorraine McDonnell

Panelists:
Rae Ann Kelsch, North Dakota State Representative
Scott Montgomery, Council of Chief State School Officers

Noon **Session 1 Central Themes**
Lorraine McDonnell

12:15 pm **Lunch**

SESSION 2: ESTIMATING COSTS TO STATES

Providing a framework for considering costs of state standards and accountability systems and applying that framework to developing empirical estimates in Florida, North Dakota, and Texas.

Framing Questions

1. What are the major activities states undertake to develop and maintain a standards-based K-12 education system? What is the nature of the costs to states associated with each of these major activities?
2. What are the sources of variation in these costs by state?
3. What are the costs associated with each major activity across select states?
4. How much do state cost estimates vary for each activity?
5. What are the conceptual and technical issues involved in developing empirical estimates of these costs?

1:15 pm **Introduction and Goals for Session**
Lauress (Laurie) Wise, HumRRO

1:30 pm **What States Do to Implement Standards-Based K-12 Education: Toward a Framework for Estimating State Costs**
Margaret (Peg) Goertz, University of Pennsylvania

1:50 pm **Developing Empirical Estimates of State Costs: Results from Florida, North Dakota, and Texas**
Douglas Harris, University of Wisconsin, Madison
Lori Taylor, Texas A&M University

2:30 pm **Break**

2:45 pm **Moderated Discussion, Part 1: Research and Business Perspectives**
Moderator: Laurie Wise

Panelists:
Thomas Toch, Education Sector
Susan Traiman, Business Roundtable

3:30 pm **Break**

3:45 pm **Moderated Discussion, Part 2: Policy and Practice Perspectives**
Moderator: Laurie Wise

Panelists:
David Driscoll, National Assessment Governing Board
R. Mark Harris, Human Capital Strategies

4:30 pm **Session 2 Central Themes**
Laurie Wise

4:45 pm **End of Formal Agenda for Day**

5:00 pm **Reception**

6:00 pm **Dinner**

FRIDAY, JANUARY 18, 2008

8:00 am **Continental Breakfast**

SESSION 3: ANALYZING STATE STANDARDS

Assessing the similarities and differences across K-12 state content and performance standards in core academic subject areas.

Framing Questions

1. How and to what extent do K-12 state content standards vary in English/language arts, mathematics, and science at key grades?
2. How and to what extent do K-12 state performance standards vary in English/language arts, mathematics, and science at key grades?
3. How and to what extent does the implementation of K-12 state content and performance standards in classrooms vary in multiple academic subjects?

8:30 am **Introduction and Goals for Session**
Thomas Corcoran, Teachers College

8:45 am **Comparing State Content Standards: Topical Coverage and Cognitive Demand in Grades 4 and 8 Reading, Mathematics, and Science in Select States**
Andrew (Andy) Porter, University of Pennsylvania
John Smithson, University of Wisconsin

9:15 am **Comparing State Performance Standards: Results from Two Recent Studies**
Peggy G. Carr, National Center for Education Statistics
Michael Petrilli, Thomas B. Fordham Foundation

10:00 am **Moderated Discussion, Part 1: Research Perspectives**
Moderator: Tom Corcoran

Panelists:
William Schmidt, Michigan State University
Barbara Reys, University of Missouri

10:45 am **Break**

11:00 am **Moderated Discussion, Part 2: Policy and Practice Perspectives**
Moderator: Tom Corcoran

Panelists:
Peter McWalters, Rhode Island Commissioner of Education
Roy Romer, Strong American Schools Campaign

11:45 am **Session 3 Central Themes**
Tom Corcoran

BREAKOUT GROUPS: LOOKING ACROSS ISSUES

Developing ideas from across the three sessions in small, mixed-role groups.

Noon **Working Lunch in Breakout Groups**
Goals, Introductions, Brainstorming

12:30 pm **Break-out Group Moderated Discussions**

1:45 pm **Reporting Out**
Group Moderators

2:15 pm **Wrap-Up of Workshop 1: Reflections on Workshop Themes**
Moderator: Lorraine McDonnell

Panelists:
Robert Linn, University of Colorado
William Tate, Washington University in St. Louis
Karen Wixson, University of Michigan

3:00 pm **Looking Ahead to Workshop 2: Outstanding Issues and Questions**
Judith Rizzo

3:30 pm **Adjourn**

PARTICIPANTS

Allison Armour-Garb, Education Studies, Rockefeller Institute of Government
Alix Beatty, Center for Education, The National Academies
Ilene Berman, Education Division, National Governors Association Center for Best Practices
Peggy G. Carr, National Center for Education Statistics, U.S. Department of Education
Betty Carvellas, Teacher Advisory Council, The National Academies
Michael Casserly, Council of the Great City Schools
Thomas Corcoran, CPRE, Teachers College, Columbia University
Stephanie Dean, The Hunt Institute
David Driscoll, National Assessment Governing Board
Kelly Duncan, Center for Education, The National Academies
Stuart Elliott, Center for Education, The National Academies
Mark Emblidge, Virginia Board of Education
William Ewell, The Hunt Institute
Michael Feuer, Division of Behavioral and Social Sciences and Education, The National Academies
Catherine Freeman, Division of Behavioral and Social Sciences and Education, The National Academies
Michael Gilligan, The Hunt Institute
Margaret E. Goertz, Graduate School of Education, University of Pennsylvania
Steven Gorman, National Center for Education Statistics, U.S. Department of Education
Lisa Guckian, The Hunt Institute
Ferrel Guillory, The Hunt Institute
Daria Hall, The Education Trust
Douglas N. Harris, Educational Policy Studies, University of Wisconsin at Madison
R. Mark Harris, Human Capital Strategies, LLC
Margaret Hilton, Center for Education, The National Academies
Barbara Kapinus, National Education Association
Rae Ann Kelsch, North Dakota State Representative
Judy Koenig, Center for Education, The National Academies
Andrew Kolstad, National Center for Education Statistics, U.S. Department of Education
Barnett A. (Sandy) Kress, Akin Gump Stauss Hauer & Feld LLP
Stephanie Levin, CPRE, Graduate School of Education, University of Pennsylvania
Dane Linn, National Governors Association

Robert L. Linn, Department of Education, University of Colorado at Boulder
Bethany Little, Alliance for Excellent Education
Diane Massell, Consortium for Policy Research in Education, University of Michigan
Lorraine M. McDonnell, Department of Political Science, University of California, Santa Barbara
Gregory F. McGinity, The Broad Foundation
Peter McWalters, Rhode Island Department of Education
Talia Milgrom-Elcott, Carnegie Corporation
Scott Montgomery, Council of Chief State School Officers
Patricia Morison, Center for Education, The National Academies
Lynn Olson, *Education Week*
Michael Petrilli, Thomas B. Fordham Foundation
Morgan Polikoff, Policy, Management and Evaluation, University of Pennsylvania
Andy Porter, Graduate School of EducationUniversity of Pennsylvania
Suellen Reed, Indiana Department of Education
Michael Resnick, National School Boards Association
Barbara J. Reys, Learning Teaching and Curriculum, University of Missouri
Judith Rizzo, The Hunt Institute
Roy Romer, Strong American Schools Campaign
Ian Rosenblum, Governor's Office of Pennsylvania
William Schmidt, Michigan State University
Sheila R. Schultz, Educational Policy Impact Center, Human Resources Research Organization
John Smithson, Measures of the Enacted Curriculum, University of Wisconsin at Madison
Brian Stecher, RAND Corporation
William Tate, Department of Arts and Sciences, Washington University in St. Louis
Lori Taylor, Bush School of Government, Texas A&M University
Thomas Toch, Education Sector
Lisa Towne, Center for Education, The National Academies
Susan Traiman, Education and Workforce Policy, Business Roundtable
Ruth Wattenberg, American Federation of Teachers
Lauress (Laurie) Wise, Human Resources Research Organization
Karen K. Wixson, School of Education, University of Michigan

Appendix B

March 2008 Workshop Agenda and Participants

Workshop on Evaluating the Options for Common Standards
March 17-18, 2008

AGENDA

MONDAY, MARCH 17, 2008

8:00 am **Continental Breakfast**

8:30 am **Introduction and Goals of Workshop Series**
Michael Feuer, National Research Council Division of Behavioral and Social Sciences and Education
Judith Rizzo, James B. Hunt, Jr. Institute for Educational Leadership and Policy
Lorraine McDonnell, University of California Santa Barbara, Workshop Series Steering Committee Chair

9:00 am **Summary of Workshop 1: Assessing the Role of K-12 Academic Standards in States**

SESSION 1: OPTIONS AND EVALUATION CRITERIA FOR COMMON STANDARDS

The session will outline a framework for considering the options related to common standards, along with a set of criteria for evaluating those options. In each case, an initial framework will be presented and then workshop participants will consider whether additional elements should be added to the framework. The options and evaluation frameworks will then be used to structure the discussion throughout the rest of the workshop.

9:30 am **Options and Evaluation Frameworks**
Stuart Elliott, National Research Council, Workshop Series Co-Study Director

Moderated Discussion
Moderator: Lorraine McDonnell

10:15 am **Break**

SESSION 2: BACKGROUND ANALYSES FOR EVALUATION CRITERIA

The session will provide background analyses related to the evaluation criteria outlined in Session 1.

10:30 am **Analyzing the Quality of Content Standards**
Karen Wixson, University of Michigan & Workshop Series Steering Committee

11:00 am **Analyzing the Impact of Standards on Teaching and Learning**

Evidence About the Impact of Standards
Douglas Harris, University of Wisconsin, Madison

Relationship of State Proficiency Standards to NAEP Score Means and Score Gains
Lauress (Laurie) Wise, HumRRO & Workshop Series Steering Committee

Moderated Discussion
Moderator: Karen Wixson

Noon **Lunch**

1:00 pm **Analyzing the Impact of Standards on Costs**

The Resource Costs of Standards, Assessments, and Accountability: Cost Implications of a Common System
Douglas Harris
Lori Taylor, Texas A&M University

Adequacy Estimates and the Implications of Common Standards for the Cost of Instruction
Lori Taylor

Moderated Discussion
Moderator: Karen Wixson

2:00 pm **Analyzing the Feasibility of Common Standards**

Assessing the Political Feasibility of Common Standards
Lorraine McDonnell

Implications of Common Standards for Adequacy Lawsuits
Goodwin Liu, University of California, Berkeley

Moderated Discussion
Moderator: Robert Linn, University of Colorado and Workshop Series Steering Committee

3:15 pm **Break**

SESSION 3: ROUNDTABLE ON APPLYING OPTIONS AND EVALUATION FRAMEWORKS TO CASES

The roundtable discussion will look at the examples of Achieve and the New England Common Assessment Program (NECAP) to consider how the options and evaluation frameworks apply to those cases.

3:30 pm **Roundtable Discussion**
Moderator: Laurie Wise
Matthew Gandal, Achieve, Inc.
Peter McWalters, Rhode Island Commissioner of Education

Moderated Discussion

5:00 pm **Adjourn**

5:15 pm **Reception**

6:00 pm **Dinner**

TUESDAY, MARCH 18, 2008

8:00 am **Continental Breakfast**

SESSION 4: APPLYING THE EVALUATION CRITERIA TO THE OPTIONS

The session will evaluate the advantages and disadvantages of the different options for common standards, using the option and evaluation frameworks from Session 1.

8:30 am **Evaluating the Options: Researcher Perspectives**
Andrew Isaacs, University of Chicago
Brian Rowan, University of Michigan
William Schmidt, Michigan State University

Moderated Discussion
Moderator: Robert Linn

10:15 am **Break**

10:30 am **Evaluating the Options: Elected Official Perspectives**
Julie Bell, National Council of State Legislators
Rae Ann Kelsch, North Dakota State Representative
Governor Roy Romer, Strong American Schools Campaign

Moderated Discussion

Noon **Lunch**

1:00 pm **Evaluating the Options: Implementer Perspectives**
David Driscoll, former Education Commissioner of Massachusetts
James Liebman, New York City Public Schools
Richard Patz, CTB/McGraw-Hill

Moderated Discussion

2:30 pm **Synthesizing the Evaluation of Options for Common Standards**
Moderator: Lorraine McDonnell
Lynn Olson, *Education Week*

3:00 pm **Concluding Reflections**
Governor James Hunt

3:30 pm **Adjourn**

PARTICIPANTS

Allison Armour-Garb, Education Studies, Rockefeller Institute of Government
Alix Beatty, Center for Education, The National Academies
Julie Bell, National Conference of State Legislatures
Ilene Berman, Education Division, National Governors Association Center for Best Practices
Sue Carnell, Michigan Governor Education Advisor
Michael Casserly, Council of the Great City Schools
Stephanie Dean, The Hunt Institute
David Driscoll, National Assessment Governing Board
Kelly Duncan, Center for Education, The National Academies
Stuart Elliott, Center for Education, The National Academies
Mark Emblidge, Virginia Board of Education
William Ewell, The Hunt Institute
Michael Feuer, Division of Behavioral and Social Sciences and Education, The National Academies
Matthew Gandal, Achieve, Inc.
Michael Gilligan, The Hunt Institute
Ferrel Guillory, The Hunt Institute
Douglas N. Harris, Educational Policy Studies, University of Wisconsin at Madison
R. Mark Harris, Human Capital Strategies, LLC
Margaret Hilton, Center for Education, The National Academies
Lindsay Hunsicker, Senate Education Committee
Governor James B. Hunt, The Hunt Institute
Andy Isaacs, University of Chicago
Barbara Kapinus, National Education Association
Rae Ann Kelsch, North Dakota State Representative
Barnett A. (Sandy) Kress, Akin Gump Stauss Hauer & Feld LLP
Jim Liebman, New York City Schools
Dane Linn, National Governors Association
Robert L. Linn, Department of Education, University of Colorado at Boulder
Bethany Little, Alliance for Excellent Education
Goodwin Liu, University of California at Berkeley Law School
Lorraine M. McDonnell, Department of Political Science, University of California, Santa Barbara
Gregory F. McGinity, The Broad Foundation
Jamie McKee, The Bill & Melinda Gates Foundation
Peter McWalters, Rhode Island State Superintendent
Scott Montgomery, Council of Chief State School Officers
Patricia Morison, Center for Education, The National Academies

Jill Morningstar, House Education and Labor Committee
Edward Nolan, Member of the NRC Teacher Advisory Council
Lynn Olson, *Education Week*
Richard J. Patz, CTB/McGraw-Hill
Morgan Polikoff, Policy, Management, and Evaluation, University of Pennsylvania
Diane Ravitch, New York University
Michael Resnick, National School Boards Association
Judith Rizzo, The Hunt Institute
Roberto Rodriguez, Senate Health, Education, Labor, and Pensions Committee
Roy Romer, Strong American Schools Campaign
Brian Rowan, University of Michigan
William Schmidt, Michigan State University
Sheila R. Schultz, Education Policy Impact Center, Human Resources Research Organization
Theresa (Teri) Siskind, Division of Accountability, South Carolina Department of Education
Lori Taylor, Bush School of Government, Texas A&M University
Thomas Toch, Education Sector
Lisa Towne, Center for Education, The National Academies
Susan Traiman, Education and Workforce Policy, Business Roundtable
Ruth Wattenberg, American Federation of Teachers
Bob Wise, Alliance for Excellent Education
Lauress (Laurie) Wise, Human Resources Research Organization
Karen K. Wixson, School of Education, University of Michigan